MIDDLE EASTERN COOKING

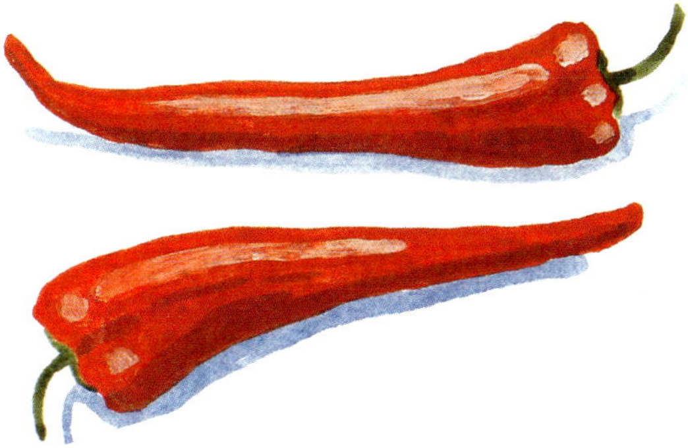

By Claudia Roden
Illustrated by Julia Binfield

SAINSBURY · WALKER BOOKS

For Cesar, my father, with love

SAINSBURY CLASSIC COOKBOOKS

Series editor: Jill Norman

Designer: Jim Bunker

Published exclusively for
J Sainsbury plc
Stamford Street London SE1 9LL
by Walker Books Ltd
184-192 Drummond Street
London NW1 3HP

First published 1986

Printed in Italy

ISBN 0-7445-0653-0

CONTENTS

INTRODUCTION

Three years ago, after two years of cookery teaching, I found myself feeling stale and starved of inspiration. My Egyptian childhood to which I had often referred seemed a figment of my imagination. I longed to be immersed again in the world of bazaars and minarets – to hear the call of the muezzin and to be followed by the smells of the spice street. So when my children went to university I set off, too, in the direction of the Middle East, in search of recipes. I made many discoveries during a series of trips, and some have come into this book to join other classics. They belong to a sensuous type of cooking where the flavours of olive oil, onion, garlic, mint and lemon and the more exotic ones of tamarind*, pomegranate and the essence of flowers come into play and where herbs are used abundantly and spices delicately.

Herodotus wrote that Arabia was scented with spices and exhaled a marvellous sweet odour. The reason for this is that it was part of the spice route. Since early times the Middle East was the transit area and the camel and caravan route for the spices which were transported from the Far East and Central Africa to Europe. The middlemen succumbed to the attractions of their highly prized merchandise. Each country adopted special favourites and combinations which characterize regional cooking today. A certain magic still surrounds the use of spices and aromatics, which are not only used for their taste but also for their medicinal, therapeutic and supposedly aphrodisiac qualities.

The countries of the Middle East have shared their past and this has given unity to their kitchen. The spread of Islam was the most important factor in the development of a gastronomic tradition comparable with that of France and China. The death of the prophet Muhammad in the year AD 632 was followed by victorious wars waged by the followers of his faith. Bedouin Arabs burst out of the Arabian Peninsula, conquered one area after another and converted it to Islam. The establishment of an enormous Islamic Empire stretching across Asia, North Africa, Spain and Sicily brought about great marriages of cooking styles and refinements in eating habits. The Turkish Ottoman empire, which expanded over an enormous territory from the 14th century until the 20th, produced a new cuisine which amalgamated the old dishes with new ones.

As a result, dishes such as skewered meats

**For more detailed information about words marked with an asterisk, see glossary p. 88.*

cooked over charcoal; stews with vegetables and fruit; vegetables stuffed with meat or rice, or both; savoury pies made with paper-thin dough filled with cheese, spinach or meat; cold vegetables cooked in oil; omelettes thick with vegetables; meat balls; rice pilafs; milk puddings with rice; nut-filled pastries soaked in syrup and syrupy fritters have been passed around and form the theme of many a local variation.

Another thing which all the countries have in common is the great value they attach to food. When I was in Turkey I asked several people why that was so. A chef in Istanbul said that it had to do with love: 'A woman shows her love by cooking well and when a man eats well he is good at making love.' In rural Anatolia a man explained: 'What gives us most pleasure in life is being hospitable, and to be hospitable you have to give food.' In the most hospitable part of the world the best food is home cooking, for life is about family and friends and pressing food on them when they visit.

With all the similarities, it is the differences and the great regional diversity which makes the cooking of the Middle East such a many-splendoured thing. For every city and every village has its own special dishes, its own favourite flavourings and makes loving use of what grows locally. They use different pots, make different fires, some cut things small while others leave them whole, some fry and some bake.

I have included recipes from several countries in this book, mostly from Turkey, Syria and the Lebanon, Iran, Egypt, Morocco and Tunisia, which have the best cuisines. Some of the dishes are famous classics, but many are little-known regional versions which I have picked because they are what we are all looking for – interesting and flavoursome, light, fresh and healthy, and also simple and easy. Most are quick to make; the more elaborate are for entertaining. All the ingredients are available. On the whole I have reduced the amount of fat and sometimes used oil instead of butter. I have simplified a few recipes but otherwise have left them as they are. Although the dishes are of different styles they are close enough to go well together and even complement each other, and you can also try one or two with your usual foods – they are easy to like.

With their happy mix of grains, pulses, seeds, nuts and vegetables it is the kind of food which fits perfectly with today's ideas of healthy eating.

Claudia Roden

REGIONAL CUISINES

Regional differences do not have much to do with national boundaries (which in some cases are relatively recent), and depend more on geography and history as well as on local produce. Dishes belong to town or country, mountain, plain or coast, and there is sometimes more in common between the cities of different countries than there is with their nearby villages. This has to do with the centres of power and the network of influence of the days of the great local empires.

The cooking can be broadly divided into four great styles:

Iranian cooking is the oldest and many of the refined and grand dishes of the entire Middle East originate in ancient Persia. Its greatest influence is on the cooking of Iraq and, more surprisingly, of Morocco. It is exquisite, marries many very different ingredients and makes use of a wide range of herbs, spices and flavourings. It is based on and around rice which can be said to be the best in the world, with long and slowly simmered soups, stews and sauces where all kinds of vegetables, pulses (yellow split peas are favourites), nuts and remarkably fresh and dried fruits, are cooked with meat or chicken. The main herbs are dill weed, mint, coriander* and parsley. Cinnamon, allspice, nutmeg, ginger and saffron or turmeric are used together – the last two giving delicate shades of yellow and orange. The sharp flavours of sour pomegranates* and tamarind*, dried limes* and sumac* are sometimes balanced with a little sweetness. Yogurt goes into many dishes.

Arab cooking is the cooking of Syria, the Lebanon, Jordan and Egypt, and can be found in most of the Arab countries. It is at its best in Syria where Aleppo is considered the great gastronomic city, and in the Lebanon which is one of the only two Middle Eastern countries to have developed a restaurant trade (the other is Turkey). It is the Lebanon, with its migrating cooks and restaurateurs, which has brought the grilled meats and appetizers of the restaurant menu to the attention of the world. But this is very limited in comparison with the wide range of home cooking based on wheat and rice and an abundance of vegetables. The flavours of onion and garlic, lemon, mint and fresh coriander* predominate, and chick-peas and sesame meal (tahina*) go into many dishes. Cinnamon is mixed with allspice, cumin with coriander* and sumac* and cardamom are used. Occasionally you detect such flavours as tamarind* or bitter oranges. Pine nuts appear often and ground almonds are used to thicken sauces.

North African (Maghrebi) cooking is scented and colourful and full of contrasts like the sharp light in the sun – hot and spicy and also sweet with sugar and honey. Couscous*, of Berber origin, is the national dish. The food of Morocco is the richest and most varied – it vies with Turkish cuisine as the third best in the world after French and Chinese. There is hardly any Ottoman influence, but a great similarity with the cooking of ancient Iran and medieval Baghdad and strong influence from Spanish Andalusia. The bourgeois cooking of Fez is the dominant cuisine. It is delicate and hardly hot; with pepper and cumin only in appetizers, and much cinnamon, saffron and ginger, mint and fresh coriander*. The cuisines of Tetouan and Marrakesh are also renowned. Tunisian food is underrated. It has the most wonderful salads, fish and egg dishes.

Classic Turkish cooking was developed in Istanbul during the Ottoman Empire. Although there is great regional diversity in home cooking throughout Turkey, professional chefs offer the same menu of saray (palace) cooking in restaurants up and down the country. They mostly come from the same region of Bolu in central Anatolia and are nearly all descended from the cooks at the sultan's kitchens (when the empire declined they went abroad or opened restaurants). This Ottoman cuisine – with its kebabs, stuffed vegetables and savoury pies, its vegetables cooked in oil, and its walnut sauces, its plaki dishes and multi-layered pastries – can be found in all the countries from the Danube to the tip of the Arabian Peninsula, from the Balkans to the shores of North Africa and also in parts of the USSR.

Devoid of any extremes of taste, the natural flavour of ingredients is embellished only by herbs, olive oil, lemon juice, yogurt and a few delicate aromatics. There are very few spices apart from cinnamon, allspice and red pepper.

UTENSILS

When I travelled across Morocco I was told by everyone that the best way to cook with the most delicious results was in unglazed earthenware pots over a charcoal fire. Second best was in tinned copper on gas, and last was in aluminium. But every kitchen I went to, like the hardware stalls at the market, was full of enormous aluminium pots and pans.

You do not have to have special equipment or utensils to cook Middle Eastern dishes. Large heavy-bottomed frying pans and saucepans (stainless steel is easiest to maintain), oven trays and casseroles are all you really need plus the usual sharp knives, wooden spoons, grater, slotted spoon, sieve or colander for washing rice, cracked wheat* and pulses, and a few special gadgets such as skewers for kebabs and courgette hollowers (a long apple corer will do).

But there is something very pleasing about using traditional equipment to make and serve the food in. So here are a few utensils you might look for on your travels. Some are already available here.

A Moroccan tagine, called tagine slaoui because they are made in the town of Salé, is a shallow round earthenware pot with a high conical lid in which stews are simmered slowly and long. It can be put straight on top of the fire but be sure not to put it on completely dry – there must always be a little water or there is a risk of cracking. Egyptians have a deeper pot they call a tagen.

A couscousière (this is the French name) can be in unglazed earthenware or in copper lined with tin. The usual ones in aluminium are perfectly good. The lower part of the pot is to cook the stew in. The upper part, with a perforated bottom, holds the grain which is steamed in the aromatic vapours of the stew. This pot is not really necessary when you are using pre-cooked couscous* but it is fun to use. In this case the grain is ready very quickly – just as soon as the steam comes through.

An ibrik for making Turkish coffee, little coffee cups and a brass tray.

A **brazier** or **barbecue**, and **skewers.**

A pestle and mortar. A food processor will do almost all the same tasks.

An Iranian rice pan with a raffia lid covered by a removable cloth called a damkoni. A non-stick pan (to unmould the rice easily) with a cloth stretched underneath the lid to catch the steam is a perfect alternative. Electric Japanese rice pots, which are now popular with Iranians interested in ease and speed, can be used too.

COOK'S TIPS

Dealing with aubergines: it is usual to sprinkle aubergines, cut in pieces or sliced, with salt and to leave them to degorge their juices in a colander. Or they are soaked for about 1 hour in salted water. After that they are rinsed and very gently squeezed or patted dry with a cloth. This is to get rid of the bitter juices and to make them absorb less oil when they are fried. The process is not always necessary because the bitterness of many aubergines is often pleasant and the oil can be gently mopped up by pressing with kitchen paper. There is little advantage in salting them when you are braising or stewing.

About soaking and cooking beans, lentils and chick-peas: years ago pulses took hours to boil and long soaking (usually overnight) was necessary to cut the cooking time. These days they cook more quickly because of new processing techniques and because the time they take to arrive in the kitchen after they are picked and dried is shorter. But it is still worth soaking them for about 1 hour – after picking them over for little stones and impurities. Drain, then cook them in fresh water or drop them in a stew or soup. Make sure the beans boil for 10 minutes before simmering. It is best (though the difference it makes is slight) to add salt when they have already begun to soften because salt retards their softening.

About rice: it is the urban staple of the Arab countries and Turkey (cracked wheat* is the rural staple) and served at almost every meal. There are many different kinds. Basmati rice which has a unique flavour and aroma and cooks always with separate grains is the closest you can find to the fine-grained varieties of Iran and Iraq. Long grain rice and a smaller oval rice is the kind you will find elsewhere. The latter is used especially for stuffing vegetables because it sticks together. The cooking time, pre-soaking and amount of water used, which vary from the same (this is how I like it) to 2½ times the volume of rice, depend on the kind of rice and whether it is preferred dry, separate and firm, or very soft and slightly moist. Ways of cooking vary in different countries and there is an incredible variety of rice dishes.

About spices: all the spices that you need are available here. People in the Middle East are not usually as fussy as the Indians about roasting and grinding their own. There are those who like to buy them whole and pulverize them with a pestle and mortar (a coffee grinder does the job very well too) – and that of course gives wonderful fresh results, but many also get their supplies already ground from specialist merchants.

A few words about saffron (*zafaran*) – because of its great cost, different kinds are used depending on the dish. The real threads are used for very delicate dishes (a different variety sold in Egypt which gives

colour only is not worth buying, so smell it first). A cheaper saffron powder (it is sometimes also combined with a few threads) has a little less of the magnificent flavour and aroma but more colour, and is used in dishes where several flavourings come into play. There is a colouring powder available here in Indian shops which gives the beautiful saffron colour and nothing else. Sometimes turmeric (*corcom*) is referred to as saffron. In Morocco that is what the poor and the street vendors use to make their foods yellow.

About oils and cooking fats: olive oil is used for dishes to be eaten cold and for fish. In Tunisia and Turkey olive oil is used for hot dishes too, but elsewhere it is groundnut, corn, cotton seed, sesame and all kinds of vegetable oils.

In this book I have not specified the kind of oil for cooking hot dishes. What I actually use and what I recommend is either sunflower or safflower and also grape seed because they do not have a strong flavour and because they are healthiest. I have often, where it does not spoil the dish, replaced butter or clarified butter, which are common cooking fats, with these oils. (Concentrated clarified butter is available in 200 g tubs.)

WHAT TO DRINK WITH MIDDLE EASTERN FOOD

Arak (or *raki*), the aniseed-flavoured aperitif distilled from grapes (in Morocco there is *mahia* made with figs and dates) is served with appetizers. Beer, too, and whisky are drunk with appetizers and with grilled foods. For those who will not have alcohol, the usual drinks besides iced water are chilled yogurt beaten with water or soda, or fresh fruit juice.

But a Middle Eastern meal is greatly enhanced by wine (due to the prohibitions of Islam, local wines are for export rather than for the domestic market). Because the food is strongly flavoured and aromatic it needs simple robust wine with character and quality which can stand up to the amalgam of flavours and support them, not great or complex wine. So do not buy anything expensive.

As usual, you can serve white wine with fish and red with meat. Buy a dry fresh white and a robust and earthy red. Sweetness in foods will make a thin dry wine too acid and sour foods will turn it flat, but a young vigorous wine with rough fruit will go well with sour, sweet and savoury dishes. A fruity-flavoured wine will also complement the fruit in a meat or chicken stew. When the dessert is fruit or a

delicate pudding you can have a dessert wine, but no wine will be sweet enough for a pastry soaked in syrup, so serve Turkish coffee instead (p. 87).

SERVING MIDDLE EASTERN FOOD

Middle Eastern food customs are related to religious holidays and festivities, to the traditions of visiting and the obligations of hospitality, to shopping at the souk for seasonal ingredients and indeed to everything that is everyday life in that part of the world.

There are still traditional households where people sit on a divan or on cushions at low round tables – large metal trays on folding wooden legs – and eat with their hands (the three fingers of the right hand) from the serving plate. There are still receptions where a succession of dishes – roast lamb, pies, meat stews, poultry, grains, and different kinds of vegetables, puddings and pastries – follow one another, and where scented water is poured from a silver ewer into a basin for guests to wash their hands while incense burns in a little holder. And there are buffets where dozens of appetizers jostle for space on the table.

Village life still revolves around the rhythm of the seasons – the milling of the grain, the drying of vegetables and fruit and the making of preserves in preparation for winter – while pots are sent to cook in the ashes at the public oven and meats are roasted over charcoal.

The recipes collected in this book are from different countries, and although these countries have much in common, they are very different in their manner of eating and serving, so there is not much point in giving strict rules about it.

The best way to use the dishes is as you would your own, in a three course meal or as snacks or for a buffet. They will represent a small but wonderful taste of a very large repertoire of cooking.

A NOTE ON THE RECIPES

I have given quite precise quantities in the recipes; they are meant to be used as a guide. You are encouraged to taste often and to use your own judgement, especially when it comes to flavouring. That is what cooking is about.

For herbs I have mentioned bunches rather than giving weights, because the amount used is so much a matter of personal discretion and will not spoil the dish. As a rule, a 'bunch' or a 'good bunch' of parsley or coriander weighs about 1 oz/25 g and a 'large' one weighs about 2 oz/50 g.

Ovens are always preheated.

1
SOUPS

Soups are not usually part of a Middle Eastern menu. A soup is more likely to be served alone as the meal itself with bread to dip in.

On cold winter days heartwarming meaty soups, which are almost as rich as stews, are prepared with different vegetables and pulses and also with dried fruit.

Offal and tripe soups are eaten for breakfast. A familiar sight at the souk is a bubbling cauldron with vegetables and a sheep's head and feet waiting for the early morning merchants.

Soups are also for special occasions and there are national soups and soups traditionally sold in the street.

The Moroccan bean soup, harira, is eaten throughout the thirty days of Ramadan.

The Turkish tripe soup which is said to be good for people with a hangover is served late at night and in the morning in special tripe soup restaurants.

Chicken broth with rice is given to the sick, barley soup is served to guests on the occasion of a baby's first tooth. And there are special wedding soups.

The soups I have included can be served as a first course for any kind of meal or the more substantial ones will provide a whole meal in the Middle Eastern manner.

ALGERIAN EGG AND LEMON SOUP

SHORBA BEIDA

This is more substantial than the usual egg and lemon soup which you can find almost everywhere in the area.

SERVES 6

18 chicken wings	*salt*
1 large onion, chopped	*4 oz/125 g vermicelli*
4 oz/125 g chick-peas, soaked for 1 hour	*a bunch of parsley, finely chopped*
½ teaspoon cinnamon	*2 egg yolks*
pepper	*juice of 1 lemon*

Put the wings in a large saucepan with the onion and drained chick-peas and pour in 4 pt/2.4 litres water. Bring to the boil, remove any scum, then add cinnamon and pepper and simmer, covered, for 1 hour or until the chick-peas are soft. Remove the wing tips and, if you like, the skin and bones too.

Add salt and vermicelli and cook for 10 minutes longer. Add the parsley and turn off the heat.

The last step, which thickens the broth, must be done just before serving. Heat the soup again. Beat the egg yolks with the lemon juice in a large bowl, then beat in 2 ladlefuls of broth. Pour this back into the saucepan, stirring vigorously. Remove from the heat quickly before the yolks curdle.

ALGERIAN FISH SOUP

SHORBA BIL HOUT

Any fish will do for this creamy spicy soup. Saffron powder which you can add, if you wish, gives it a brilliant yellow colour and a delicious aroma.

SERVES 6

2 onions, chopped
4 tablespoons olive oil
6 cloves garlic, crushed
2 large potatoes, cubed
1 lb/500 g tomatoes, peeled and diced
salt and pepper
2 bay leaves
½ teaspoon thyme
¼ teaspoon saffron powder (optional)
1½ teaspoons harissa (or to taste)*
or
1½ teaspoons paprika and a good pinch of cayenne
2 lb/1 kg fillet of cod or haddock, skin and bones removed
juice of ½-1 lemon
2 eggs

Soften the onion in oil in a large pan. Add the garlic and let it just begin to colour.

Add the rest of the ingredients except the fish, lemon juice and eggs. Cover with 4 pt/2.4 litres water and simmer for 15 minutes or until the potatoes are soft.

Put the fish in and cook for 7 minutes or until it begins to flake.

Take out the bay leaves and put the soup through the blender. Return it to the pan, add the lemon juice and taste. Adjust seasonings if necessary. Add water if the soup is too thick.

Just before serving, beat the eggs, add a ladleful of soup, beat well and pour into the simmering soup, stirring vigorously.

Turn off the heat at once so that the eggs thicken the soup but do not curdle.

Tunisian Fish Soup

BROUDOU BIL HOUT

This is so rich it is a meal in itself – more like a stew and it is easy enough to make in large quantities. Use a mixture of fish and seafood; cheap, ordinary fish, if you like, for every day (it will still be good) and more unusual Mediterranean fish for a party. The choice is very large. It is good to have some firm-fleshed fish, such as monkfish, gurnard, bream or bass as well as delicate fish such as whiting, flatfish, cod or haddock. Small whole fish, pieces of eel and seafood, such as squid, prawns and crabmeat, will make a grand and attractive soup.

SERVES 12

4 lb/2 kg fish and seafood

4 onions, coarsely chopped

5 tablespoons olive oil

1 large green pepper, deseeded and chopped

1 large red pepper, deseeded and chopped

4 cloves garlic, chopped

4 large potatoes, diced

2 fennel bulbs with their leaves, diced

salt

½ teaspoon saffron powder or colouring

½-1 teaspoon ground cumin

½-1 teaspoon ground cinnamon

1 teaspoon paprika

a pinch of cayenne

juice of 1½ lemons

8 tomatoes, peeled and chopped

a large bunch of parsley, finely chopped

a large bunch of coriander, finely chopped*

Prepare the fish. Skin and bone and cut it into little pieces. If you are using small fish, gut, scale and wash them. Peel prawns and clean squid (see p. 31).

Fry the onions in oil until soft. Add the peppers and garlic. When the peppers are soft, add about

5 pt/3 litres of water. Throw in the potatoes and fennel. Add the salt, saffron, cumin, cinnamon, paprika, cayenne and the lemon juice and simmer for 30 minutes.

Then put in the prepared fish, tomatoes and herbs; add enough water to have a good amount of liquid and cook a few minutes only until the fish is done. Serve with bread.

VARIATIONS

Other possible additions are:

2 tablespoons of capers, 2 tablespoons of caraway seeds, and a teaspoon of ground coriander.

You can use harissa instead of paprika and cayenne. Put it in to taste – 1 or 2 teaspoons only to start with as it is very hot.

Instead of lemon juice you can have 2 chopped up preserved lemons.

Lentil Soup with Spinach and Lemon

ADS BI HAMUD

This is a Lebanese mountain soup.

SERVES 6

12 oz/375 g green lentils, soaked for 1 hour

salt and pepper

2 lb/1 kg spinach

2 onions, cut in half then sliced thinly

4 tablespoons oil

5 cloves garlic, sliced

1 tablespoon plain flour

juice of 1½ lemons

Wash and drain the lentils. Put them in a pan with water to cover and simmer for 30 minutes or until they are very tender, adding salt and pepper towards the end.

Wash the spinach, remove the stems and chop the leaves coarsely. Add them to the lentils.

Fry the onions in oil until soft, add the garlic, and when the aroma rises add the flour and stir well. Add a teacupful of water and stir until this sauce thickens. Pour into the soup.

Add the lemon juice and more water, if necessary, and simmer until it is a thick rich soup.

Serve very hot.

Lentil Soup

SHORBAT ADS

This homely and nourishing Egyptian soup is easy to make for a large number of people. It is very popular in our family.

SERVES 6-8

1½ large onions, coarsely chopped

2-3 tablespoons oil

3 cloves garlic, crushed

1 lb/500 g red lentils

3 pt/1.8 litres meat or chicken stock

1 teaspoon ground cumin

*1 teaspoon ground coriander**

a pinch of cayenne (optional)

salt

juice of 1 lemon

a small bunch of parsley or dill, finely chopped

Fry the onions in oil in a large pan, stirring occasionally until they are very brown. Add the garlic and stir.

Put the lentils in, then the stock and bring to the boil. Remove any scum.

Stir in the cumin, coriander and, if you like, cayenne and simmer for about 1 hour or until the lentils have disintegrated, adding the salt when they have begun to soften.

If necessary add water to thin the soup to a light cream.

Stir in the lemon juice and serve, sprinkling a little parsley or dill into each bowl.

VARIATIONS

*Add 4 oz/125 g rice or vermicelli (broken in your hands) 15 minutes before the end.

*Add 2 tomatoes, peeled and chopped, when the soup is ready and just let them soften.

*Add 1 lb/500 g spinach (wash the leaves, remove the stems and cut into shreds) and cook a further 10 minutes.

GREEN YOGURT SOUP

ASHE MAST

This lovely fresh tasting cold soup is Iranian. It is ideal for a summer day.

SERVES 6

2 large onions
3 tablespoons oil
2 tablespoons red lentils
4 oz/125 g rice
1 lb/500 g spinach
a small bunch of coriander, chopped*
a small bunch of chives, finely chopped
a small bunch of parsley, chopped
1 pt/600 ml plain yogurt
2 teaspoons dried mint

Chop 1 onion and fry in 1½ tablespoons of oil until it is soft. Add salt and pepper, the lentils and the rice. Cover with 1¾ pt/1 litre water, bring to the boil and simmer for about 20 minutes or until the pulses and rice are tender.

Add the spinach, stems removed and thoroughly washed and shredded, with the coriander, chives and parsley, and cook for about 10 minutes until the spinach is soft. Add a little more water if necessary to have enough liquid in the soup. Let it cool.

Beat the yogurt, stir it in and pour the soup into a serving bowl.

For the garnish, slice the remaining onion and fry in 1½ tablespoons of oil until golden. Add the mint and cook, stirring for a minute longer. Sprinkle over the soup.

VARIATIONS

*Serve the soup hot. I beat the yogurt in then heat it through without letting it boil so that it does not curdle. I also sometimes add the juice of 1 lemon.

*Split peas can be used instead of lentils. Boil them for 20 minutes before the rice is put in.

Algerian Bean Soup

DJARI BEL FOUL

This soup can be made quite hot and peppery.

SERVES 6

1 onion, chopped
2 tablespoons oil
8 oz/250 g white beans, soaked for 1 hour
4 pt/2.4 litres meat or chicken stock
salt and pepper
½ teaspoon harissa or a pinch of cayenne*
3 large tomatoes, peeled and chopped
4 oz/125 g vermicelli
a bunch of parsley, finely chopped

Fry the onion in oil until golden.

Add the beans and stock and cook for about 45 minutes or until the beans are tender. Then add salt and pepper, harissa or cayenne, the tomatoes and vermicelli and cook for another 10 minutes. Add the parsley and serve.

Moroccan Harira

Moroccans break the daily fast on this nutritious soup during the month-long fast of Ramadan. Late at night the signal that they can begin to eat is given – a thunder of cannon and a roll of drums. The soup is followed by music, and singing and dancing by the men. Two hours later the main meal begins and often continues until dawn.

Harira is sold in the souks at all times of day – especially at breakfast. Vendors put out tables and benches and ladle the thick broth from huge cauldrons into ornately painted bowls.

Every family has their own special recipe for this much-loved soup.

SERVES 8

8 oz/250 g chicken, preferably from the leg, diced
8 oz/250 g chick-peas, soaked for 1 hour
1 onion, coarsely chopped
8 oz/250 g tomatoes, skinned and chopped
5 pt/3 litres chicken stock
pepper
1 teaspoon ground cinnamon
salt
4 oz/125 g rice or vermicelli
a bunch of fresh coriander or parsley, finely chopped*
3 eggs, beaten
2 lemons, cut into wedges

Put the chicken, chick-peas, onion and tomatoes to boil in the stock. Remove any scum. Add the pepper and cinnamon, then simmer for about 1 hour until the chick-peas are soft, adding salt towards the end. Fifteen minutes before you want to serve, throw in the rice or vermicelli. Finally add the coriander or parsley, take the soup off the heat and beat the eggs in vigorously – they will cook enough to thicken the soup. (A flour and water paste is also used but I prefer to leave it out.) Serve hot with lemon wedges.

POMEGRANATE SOUP

ASH ANAR

The sour and treacly dark brown pomegranate syrup* (you can now buy it in bottles) combined with sugar gives this exotic Iranian soup an intriguing sweet and sour flavour.

SERVES 6

8 oz/250 g minced lamb or veal
3 onions
salt and pepper
3 tablespoons oil
4 tablespoons yellow split peas
6 tablespoons rice
a bunch of coriander, chopped*
a bunch of parsley, chopped
a bunch of mint, chopped
1 lb/500 g spinach, shredded
¼ pt/150 ml pomegranate syrup
4-5 tablespoons sugar
juice of 1 lemon

First make the meat balls.

Work the meat with 1 grated onion and a little salt and pepper and roll into balls the size of small walnuts.

Fry 2 chopped onions in oil in a large saucepan until golden. Put in the meat balls and turn to brown them all over.

Add the yellow split peas, pour in 3 pt/1.8 litres water, and simmer for 20 minutes. Throw in the rice and cook 15 minutes longer.

Add the herbs and spinach, pomegranate syrup and sugar, the lemon juice, salt and pepper and simmer for about 20 minutes or until all the ingredients are tender.

You will need to taste from time to time to achieve a delicate balance of flavourings and you may need to add water so that it is more a soup than a stew. Serve hot.

VEGETABLE AND MEAT BALL SOUP

SHORBA BEL KOFTA

This green vegetable soup with delicately spiced meat balls is Egyptian.

SERVES 6

1 large potato, diced
2 leeks, chopped
1 onion, chopped
1 stalk of celery, diced
2 cloves garlic, sliced
4 oz/125 g fresh or frozen broad beans
4 pt/2.4 litres meat or chicken stock
4 courgettes, diced
8 oz/250 g spinach, shredded
juice of 1 lemon
salt and pepper
a few sprigs of mint, finely chopped or 1 tablespoon dried mint

For the meat balls

1 lb/500 g minced veal
1 onion, grated
salt and pepper
½ teaspoon ground cinnamon
¼ teaspoon ground cardamom

Put all the soup ingredients except the courgettes, spinach and mint into a large pan and bring to the boil.

To make the meat balls, work the meat well with the grated onion, salt and pepper, cinnamon and cardamom. Shape into balls the size of large marbles.

Drop the meatballs into the soup and simmer for 30 minutes or until done, adding the courgettes, spinach and mint for the last 10 minutes. Serve hot.

VARIATIONS

*Add 2 large tomatoes, peeled and chopped.

*Throw 4 tablespoons of rice in 15 minutes before you are ready to serve.

*Throw in a handful of broken vermicelli 15 minutes before the soup is ready.

2

APPETIZERS, VEGETABLES AND SIDE DISHES

Appetizers are for entertaining and also for every day. It is usual to have a large assortment at parties, from simple ones like olives, pickles and nuts to pies, salads, purées and all kinds of miniature foods. They are presented on small individual serving plates and scattered around the room or placed on a coffee table for guests to pick at. They are meant to whet the appetite with their sharpness and spiciness, but by the time the usually late dinner arrives most people have no room left. At a family meal all the dishes are put on the table at the same time and appetizers become side dishes.

I have given many recipes in this chapter because they are so versatile. You can serve several appetizers at a time – with a variety of flavours, textures and colours – for people to have a little taste of each, or you can choose one alone as a first course. There are salads and cold vegetables, which you can offer with meat and fish, and there are egg dishes and pies which make light meals in themselves accompanied by yogurt and a fresh salad. The list could be very much longer with such things as meat balls, and fish fritters, but I have given more vegetable *mezze* because that is what I like to have myself.

Vegetables are one of the most important, and to me, the most attractive features of Middle Eastern cooking. They are cooked with meats in stews, with rice and cracked wheat* in pilafs and they go into soups. Vegetable dishes such as stuffed vegetables and vegetables cooked in oil are also served as a separate course – often to start the meal, but sometimes as the third course, after meats. I have put them all in this chapter because they make such a good first course and I did not want to divide them.

Mixed Arab Salad

SALATA BALADI

This is a very common salad throughout the Middle East. You can serve it with everything.

SERVES 6

1 small cos lettuce or ½ small white cabbage, shredded

3 firm tomatoes, diced

1 green pepper, deseeded and diced (optional)

½ cucumber, peeled or not, diced

5 spring onions or 1 mild onion, chopped

16 radishes, sliced (optional)

a bunch of parsley or coriander, coarsely chopped*

a few sprigs of mint, chopped (optional)

For the dressing

4 tablespoons olive oil

juice of 1 lemon, or more

salt and pepper

Mix all the ingredients together and dress just before serving.

VARIATIONS

**Fattoush.* Toast an opened-out pitta bread and break it into small pieces. Sprinkle over the salad.

You may add a sprinkling of sumac and a handful of pomegranate seeds.

Chick-Pea Dip

HUMMUS BI TAHINA

Serve this most popular Arab cream salad with warm pitta bread to dip in it. Accompany with a plate of radishes, spring onions and pickled cucumbers or turnips.

SERVES 4

6 oz/175 g chick-peas, soaked for at least 1 hour

*4 tablespoons tahina**

juice of 2 lemons, or to taste

4 cloves garlic, crushed (optional)

salt

2 tablespoons olive oil

+ Water + 1 level teasp Cumin

Drain and boil the chick-peas in fresh water for about 1 hour or until soft. Put them in a blender with enough of their cooking water to make a thick paste. Tasting as you go, add the tahina, lemon juice, garlic, if used, and salt and blend very thoroughly to a light cream (you may need a little more water). Spread the cream flat on a plate and sprinkle with olive oil.

VARIATION

*Add 1 teaspoon ground cumin to the cream and garnish with a sprinkling of paprika and cumin.

Parsley and Cracked Wheat Salad

TABBOULEH

The most popular – even supreme – Arab salad is a village dish of Syria and the Lebanon which became an institution when it was adopted by cafés there as an appetizer to serve with the local spirit, *arak*. Sixty years ago it was made in the mountain villages with a large proportion of wheat. These days, however, it is all green with only a speckle of buff-coloured wheat, and very sharp with plenty of lemon juice. Serve it as an appetizer, as a first course, or to accompany grilled foods. It is delicious and refreshing for a summer buffet.

SERVES 6 OR MORE

*4 oz/125 g medium-fine cracked wheat**

juice of 2 lemons, or more

salt and pepper

5 tablespoons olive oil

10 oz/300 g flat parsley, finely chopped

6 spring onions or 1 small onion, finely chopped

3 oz/75 g (1 large bunch) fresh mint, finely chopped

or 2 tablespoons dried mint, finely chopped

3 tomatoes, diced

cos lettuce leaves (from the heart), to be used as a scoop

An hour before you are ready to serve, soak the cracked wheat in cold water for about 15 minutes, then rinse in a strainer and squeeze the excess water out. Dress with the lemon juice, salt and pepper, leave to rest, and when it is plump and tender add the oil.

Chop the herbs as late as possible before you are ready to serve. It is best to do this by hand, but with such a large quantity it makes sense to use the food processor. If you do, make sure that you do not turn them into a mush. Mix with the spring onions or onion and cracked wheat. Taste and adjust the seasoning and add more lemon juice if necessary. Serve on a large flat serving dish. Sprinkle the tomatoes over the top, and dig the lettuce leaves in around the edges or serve them in a separate bowl.

Aubergine and Tahina Salad

BABA GHANOUSH

This delicious Arab purée is as popular as hummus and they are often served together. Have warm pitta bread to dip in it.

SERVES 4

1 large aubergine

juice of 2 lemons

*3 tablespoons tahina**

2 cloves garlic, crushed

salt

To garnish

a few sprigs of parsley, finely chopped

Roast the aubergine under the grill, turning it a few times until the skin is black and blistered and the flesh feels very soft when you press it. Peel the aubergine and squeeze out the juice then put it in the blender with the rest of the ingredients and 2 tablespoons of water.

Spread the cream on a flat plate and sprinkle with parsley.

STUFFED VINE LEAVES

YAPRAK DOLMASI

You can find stuffed vine leaves in every Middle Eastern country. They are eaten hot or cold, and the many different fillings combine rice with meat (those with meat are eaten hot), onions, tomatoes and all kinds of nuts, dried fruit, herbs and spices. There is one – a Lenten dish from Syria – which has a filling of cracked wheat* and split peas. They are sometimes served with a tomato or an egg and lemon sauce, and can also be popped into a stew. In the Arab world the rice is used raw; in Turkey it is cooked first.

This recipe is a classic one from Turkey. It is to be served cold as an appetizer.

SERVES 6

8 oz/250 g vine leaves
4 fl oz/125 ml olive oil
juice of 1 lemon
salt and pepper
1 teaspoon sugar

For the filling

1 lb/500 g onions, chopped
5 tablespoons olive oil
1 oz/25 g pine nuts
8 oz/250 g long grain rice
1 oz/25 g currants
salt and pepper
1 tablespoon sugar
a small bunch of mint, finely chopped
a small bunch of dill, finely chopped
a small bunch of parsley, finely chopped

If you have fresh vine leaves blanch them for a few seconds in boiling water until they are limp. With leaves preserved in brine, soak them, first in boiling water, then in 2 changes of fresh cold water for 1 hour to remove the salt.

To make the filling, fry the onions in oil until golden. Add the pine nuts and let them brown lightly. Then add the rice, washed and drained, and stir until it becomes transparent.

Add currants, salt, pepper and sugar and pour in ½ pt/300 ml water. Stir well and cook, covered, for 15 minutes then stir in the herbs.

Line the bottom of a heavy pan with torn discarded vine leaves (or lettuce leaves) to prevent the stuffed ones from sticking and burning.

To fill the vine leaves, lay a leaf on a plate, vein side up. Put 1 tablespoon of filling in a line along the stem edge. Fold this edge over it, then fold both sides in towards the centre and roll up like a small cigar. Fill the rest in the same way.

Pack the leaves tightly in layers in the pan. Pour over them a mixture of the olive oil, lemon juice, salt, pepper and sugar and enough water just to cover the leaves.

Place a small plate on top to hold the leaves down and cook covered for about 1 hour.

Let them cool in the pan before turning out.

Yogurt and Cucumber Salad

CACIK

You will find this famous Turkish salad everywhere in the Middle East.

SERVES 6

1 large cucumber, peeled and chopped
1 pt/600 ml sheep's milk or strained yogurt
salt and pepper
1-2 cloves garlic, crushed
a few sprigs of mint or dill, finely chopped or 1 tablespoon dried mint
2 tablespoons olive oil

Beat the yogurt with a little salt and pepper. Add the garlic and some of the mint or dill.

Just before you are ready to serve, mix in the cucumber.

Garnish with a dribble of olive oil and a sprinkling of herbs.

Cucumber Relish

SHLADA L'FILFIL

I call this salad a relish because it is peppery and the ingredients are chopped small. It is delightfully hot and refreshing. There is a strong Spanish influence on the cooking of Tetouan in Morocco where it comes from. Chop the tomatoes by hand, the rest can be done in a food processor but be careful not to turn everything into a mush.

SERVES 6

1 large cucumber, finely chopped
½ Spanish onion, finely chopped
2 hot chilli peppers, finely chopped
salt
3 tablespoons olive oil
2 tablespoons wine vinegar
2 large tomatoes, chopped

Mix the cucumber, onion and chillies in a colander and sprinkle with salt. Let them give up their juices for 30 minutes, then dress with olive oil and vinegar and stir in the tomatoes. Serve with bread or as an accompaniment to grilled foods.

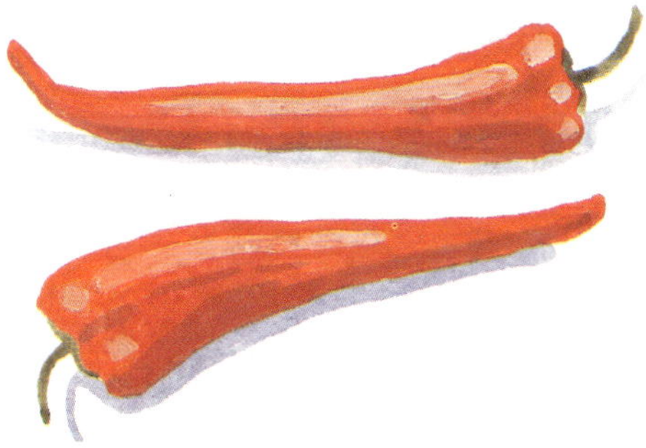

Tunisian Grilled Salad

SLATA MICHWIYA

All the vegetables – the onions included – acquire a delicious mellow flavour when they are roasted. I also like to make this salad without the last three ingredients.

SERVES 6

3 small onions

4 sweet peppers (green or a mixture with red and yellow ones)

2 large tomatoes

1 hot chilli pepper

salt

juice of 1 lemon

3-4 tablespoons olive oil

1 tablespoon capers

2 eggs, hard-boiled and cut in wedges lengthways

3½ oz/100 g can of tuna

Although the vegetables are usually cooked under the grill it is easier to roast them in the hottest possible oven. Put the onions and peppers in first and leave them for about 30 minutes or until the skins are very brown and they feel soft. Put the tomatoes in for 4 minutes. Put the roasted peppers straight into a polythene bag, close it tightly and leave them for about 10 minutes. This will make them easier to peel. Seed the peppers. Peel and cut the vegetables into small pieces. Chop the hot chilli. Mix together in a bowl, season with salt, lemon juice and oil and add the capers. Arrange on a shallow serving dish with the eggs and crumble the tuna on top.

Mashed Carrot Salad

OMI HOURIYA

This is a Tunisian salad to eat with bread. It is hot and spicy to whet the appetite. If you have some harissa* use it instead of the paprika and cayenne.

SERVES 4

1½ lb/750 g carrots

salt and pepper

4 tablespoons olive oil

3 tablespoons wine vinegar

2 cloves garlic, crushed

1 teaspoon paprika

a good pinch of cayenne

2 teaspoons cumin

To garnish

a few black olives

Scrape and boil the carrots in salted water until soft. Drain and mash them with a fork or chop them finely. Add the rest of the ingredients and serve cold, garnished with olives.

Cucumber Salad with Mint

KHIAR BIL NA'NA

This cool minty salad goes well with grills, savoury pies and omelettes.

SERVES 6

1 large cucumber

salt

juice of 1 lemon

3 tablespoons olive oil

a few sprigs of mint, finely chopped or 1 tablespoon dried mint

black pepper

Peel and slice the cucumber as thinly as possible. Sprinkle very generously with salt and leave to drain in a colander for 1 hour.

Mix the lemon juice, oil, mint and pepper, and let the herb infuse the dressing with its perfume.

Rinse the cucumber, if necessary (most of the salt will be carried away by the escaping liquid), drain well and dress.

SQUID SALAD

SALATIT MANTIQ

This is a simple Tunisian way of serving squid. Some people would stir 1 tablespoon of the peppery paste harissa* into the dressing – but I prefer it without.

SERVES 4

4 baby squid

salt

4 tablespoons olive oil

juice of 1 lemon

pepper

a small bunch of parsley, finely chopped

To clean the squid: pull the head out of the pouch and with it the soft innards and the transparent spine. Peel off the reddish membrane from the body, and rinse out the mucous membrane from inside. Sever the tentacles from the rest of the head.

Cut the body into rings ½ in/1 cm thick and the tentacles into small pieces. Poach in salted water for about 5-10 minutes. Remove from the heat and drain just as soon as the squid is tender and turns opaque. Dress with a mixture of olive oil, lemon juice and pepper. Serve cold, sprinkled with parsley.

CELERIAC AND CARROT TARATOR

TARATORLU KEREVIZ

In Turkey all sorts of boiled vegetables, including cauliflower and beans, are dressed with a nut sauce called tarator. In this recipe, celeriac and carrots make a good combination of flavour and colour and yogurt is a refreshing addition to the sauce.

SERVES 4-6

1 large celeriac

3 large carrots

salt

For the sauce

4 oz/125 g hazelnuts, coarsely ground

2 cloves garlic, crushed

4 tablespoons olive oil

3 tablespoons wine vinegar

¼ pt/150 ml natural yogurt

salt

a pinch of cayenne pepper (optional)

To garnish

a sprig of parsley, finely chopped

½ teaspoon paprika

Peel and cut the celeriac and carrots into matchsticks. Boil in salted water for a short time until just tender, and drain.

For the sauce, mix the nuts with the rest of the ingredients. Pour the sauce over the vegetables in a serving dish, and garnish with parsley and paprika.

COLD MUSSELS, TURKISH STYLE

MIDYE PILAKISI

Mussels in Turkey are particularly large and fleshy, but those available here will do very well.

SERVES 6

4 lb/2 kg mussels
1 large onion, finely chopped
4-6 tablespoons olive oil
3 cloves garlic, finely chopped
2 carrots, diced
salt and pepper
1 teaspoon sugar
2 bay leaves
2 potatoes, diced
3 tomatoes, peeled and diced
a good bunch of parsley, chopped

Scrub the mussels, pull off their beards (the stringy bit that hangs out of the shell) with a knife and wash in several waters.

Discard broken ones and those which are too heavy or too light, or which do not close when they are tapped or plunged in cold water.

Put them in a large pan with a cupful of water and the lid on. Bring the water to the boil and steam them open – it takes between 3-10 minutes.

When they are cool enough to handle, remove from their shells and set aside. Strain the liquid in the pan to get rid of any sand.

Fry the onion in oil until golden. Add the garlic and carrots and fry until the aroma rises. Then add the mussel liquid, salt and pepper, sugar and bay leaves and simmer for 15 minutes.

Now add the potatoes and tomatoes and more water to cover, if necessary, and cook another 10 minutes or until the vegetables are soft. Put the mussels in and heat through.

Let cool, transfer to a serving dish and garnish with the parsley.

LITTLE FILLO SAVOURIES WITH CHEESE AND SPINACH FILLINGS

BOREK

You can find these in most countries of the Middle East, often with their Turkish name *borek*. They come in different shapes and with a variety of fillings. There are also different ways of making the paper-thin dough, but now that fillo* is readily available you cannot do better than to use it. The sheets are sold in 1 lb/500 g packets. For years the standard packets contained 24 sheets but there are now a few different makes and the sheets vary in size and number.

As the 2 most popular fillings are spinach and cheese, and the most common shapes are cigarettes and triangles, I have given the recipe for these.

MAKES ABOUT 60

1 lb/500 g (1 packet) fillo
6 oz/175 g butter, melted

For the cheese filling

12 oz/375 g fetta cheese, mashed or farmhouse Cheddar, grated
2 eggs
pepper
2 teaspoons dried mint

For the spinach filling

2 lb/1 kg fresh spinach or 1 lb/500 g frozen whole leaf spinach
4 oz/125 g fetta, mashed or cottage cheese, well drained
salt and pepper
a good pinch of nutmeg
2 eggs

Make the fillings first.

For the cheese filling, mix the ingredients in a bowl.

For the spinach filling, wash the leaves, remove the stems, and cook them in their own juice in a pan with the lid on until they crumple, then drain well (it is usual, but not necessary, to chop the leaves coarsely). Or defrost frozen spinach and squeeze all

the water out. Mix with the rest of the ingredients (fetta will give a stronger flavour and, as it is salty, you may not need to add any salt).

Now cut the sheets of fillo into rectangular strips about 3 in/7 cm wide – this will make rather small pastries, but in the Middle East 'small is beautiful' and for entertaining that is what you want. Put the strips in a pile so that those underneath do not dry out (they do so very quickly once they are out of the packet).

To make cheese cigarettes, brush the top strip very lightly with melted butter. Put 1 heaped teaspoon of cheese filling at one end and roll up like a cigarette. Turn the ends in about a third of the way to trap the filling, then continue to roll with the sides seemingly open.

Repeat with more strips until all the filling has gone. Then place side by side on a buttered baking tray and brush the tops very lightly with butter.

To make spinach triangles, brush a strip of fillo with melted butter, put 1 heaped teaspoon of filling at one end about 1 in/2 cm from the edge and fold one corner up over it. Then fold again and again until the whole strip is folded into a small triangle (make sure you close any holes, as liquid from the filling can ooze out). Place close to each other on a buttered baking tray and brush the tops lightly with melted butter.

Bake the cheese cigarettes and spinach triangles in a preheated gas 4/350°F/180°C oven for 30 minutes or until crisp and golden. As you will have more than 1 baking tray you will have to move them around so that those underneath have a chance to get brown. Serve hot.

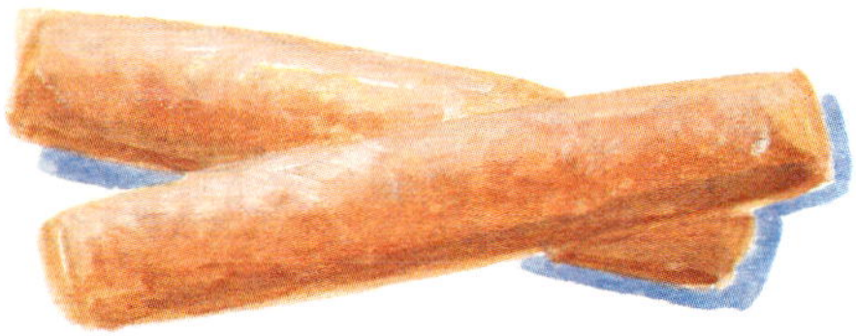

Moroccan Chicken Pie

TRID

The traditional pastry for this pie is a yeast dough kneaded for half an hour to great elasticity, rolled into balls, anointed with oil, then pulled into paper-thin sheets. I give here a simplified version and the easy alternative of using bought puff pastry. It makes a delicious pie.

SERVES 8

8 chicken drumsticks
2 lb/1 kg onions, grated or finely chopped
6 tablespoons oil
salt and pepper
2 teaspoons ground cinnamon
a good pinch of saffron powder (optional)
4 oz/125 g split blanched almonds
1 lb/500 g puff pastry
plain flour
1 egg, separated

Prepare the filling. Put the drumsticks with the onions and oil in a large pan over a very low flame. Add salt, pepper, 1½ teaspoons cinnamon and saffron, if you like, and cook gently, stirring occasionally, for about 30 minutes until the chicken is so tender that it comes off the bone (it cooks in the onion juice). Take the drumsticks out, remove the skin and bones and cut the chicken into small pieces. Continue to cook the onions, stirring often, until all the liquid has gone and they have turned into a soft golden cream, then put back the chicken pieces and take off the heat.

Toast the almonds under the grill or in a dry frying pan, and set aside.

Divide the pastry into 2 balls. Roll out the first one, thinly, on a floured surface with a floured rolling pin. Lift it up and ease it into a round oven dish or tray about 11 in/28 cm in diameter, pulling the pastry up and letting it hang a little over the sides.

Trim the edges with a knife, prick with a fork in several places, and bake blind for 15 minutes in a preheated gas 6/400°F/200°C oven (it does not matter if it puffs up). Brush with egg white and put it back in the oven for 5 minutes. This will prevent the pastry from becoming soggy with the filling.

Spread the filling inside the pastry shell and sprinkle with the almonds.

Roll out the second ball of pastry, as before, and place it on top, sealing the edges well. Brush with egg yolk and bake in a gas 4/350°F/180°C oven for 30 minutes, or until crisp and brown.

Serve hot, sprinkled with more cinnamon.

MOROCCAN MEAT PIES

BRIOUAT BEL KEFTA

In Morocco, pastry is made by dabbing a tray placed upside down over a fire with a very soft dough until a round sheet as thin as paper is formed. Bought puff pastry rolled very thin makes a quick and respectable alternative. The spicy filling is delicious. You can make it very hot with cayenne.

MAKES 8

1 lb/500 g puff pastry
2 onions, chopped
3 tablespoons oil
1 lb/500 g minced lamb or beef
salt and pepper
3 teaspoons ground cinnamon
a pinch of cayenne (optional)
a bunch of parsley, finely chopped
a bunch of coriander, finely chopped*
6 eggs, beaten
plain flour
oil for deep frying

Make the filling. Fry the onions in oil until golden. Add the meat, salt, pepper, 1½ teaspoons cinnamon and cayenne, if you like, and fry, stirring occasionally, until the meat becomes dry.

Then add the parsley and coriander and stir in the eggs. Keep stirring and cook for a minute or so until the eggs set.

Cut the pastry into 8 pieces. Make little balls and roll out, as thin as you can without breaking, on a floured surface with a floured rolling pin.

Place 2 heaped tablespoons of filling on one side near the centre of each sheet and fold into a packet. Pinch the edges together so as to close the little pies firmly.

Deep fry in not-too-hot oil until well browned, turning over once.

Drain on absorbent paper and serve very hot, sprinkled with the remaining cinnamon.

VARIATION

Do not fry the pies. Place them on a baking tray, brush the top with egg and bake in a preheated gas 5/375°F/190°C oven for 30 minutes, or until they are brown. Serve hot, sprinkled with the remaining cinnamon.

Smoked Cod's Roe Dip

TARAMASALATA

This new light and easy version of the famous smoked cod's roe cream has been adopted by a few Greek restaurants in Britain. Make it as an appetizer to dip into with pitta bread.

SERVES 4

4 oz/125 g piece of smoked cod's roe
juice of 1 lemon, or more to taste
4 oz/125 g cream cheese
½ small onion, grated (optional)

Wash the cod's roe, put it in the food processor (leave the skin on as it gives a stronger colour) with the lemon juice and blend to a smooth paste.

Add the cream cheese and blend for only a very short time so that it does not become too soft (it can become almost liquid).

Stir in the onion, if used, and serve with pitta bread cut into triangles.

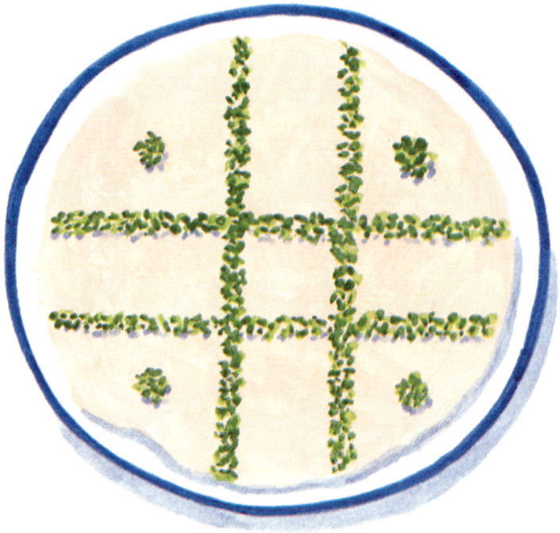

Aubergine Salad

NAZKHATOUN

This salad is from Iran.

SERVES 6

2 aubergines
2 cloves garlic, crushed
a few sprigs of mint, finely chopped or 2 teaspoons dried mint
2 tablespoons olive oil
salt and pepper
2 tablespoons sour pomegranate syrup or juice of 1 lemon*
3 tomatoes, peeled and chopped

Turn the aubergines under the grill until their skins are black and blistered, and their flesh feels soft inside. Put them in a colander and peel them as soon as they are cool enough to handle. Squeeze out the juice and chop or mash them or put through the food processor. Add the rest of the ingredients, except the tomatoes, and mix well. Fold the tomatoes in gently and serve cold.

Fried Aubergine Slices

PATLICAN TAVA

Two of the simplest and most wonderful ways of serving aubergines are Turkish. Slices cut lengthways are fried in hot oil, topped with thick yogurt or with fresh tomato sauce, and served cold.

For every day, do one or the other. But for a party it makes an attractive presentation to do both. Slice the aubergines into smaller rounds and alternate the two toppings as in a chess board.

SERVES 8-10

4 medium aubergines
salt
oil for frying

For the tomato sauce topping

1 clove garlic, crushed
1 tablespoon oil
3 large tomatoes, peeled and chopped
salt and pepper
1 tablespoon wine vinegar
2 teaspoons sugar
1 tablespoon currants (optional)
1 tablespoon pine nuts (optional)
a small bunch of parsley, finely chopped

For the yogurt topping

½ pt/300 ml sheep's milk or strained yogurt
1 clove garlic, crushed (optional)

Cut the aubergines lengthways, or in rounds, in ¼ in/5 mm thick slices. Sprinkle with salt and leave 30 minutes for the juices to degorge. Then rinse and pat dry.

Fry very quickly in hot oil turning over once until they feel soft when you prick them with a fork. Drain on kitchen paper and arrange on a flat serving dish.

To make the tomato sauce, fry the garlic in oil, add the tomatoes, salt, pepper, vinegar, sugar and, if you like, currants and cook for 2-3 minutes. Spread a little of the sauce on half the aubergine slices and sprinkle with lightly fried or toasted pine nuts, if used, and with parsley.

Cover the rest of the slices with yogurt, beaten, if you like, with a little garlic. Serve cold.

VARIATION

Here is an alternative for those who do not like frying.

Simmer the aubergine slices in a mixture of tomato juice and water for about 20 minutes until they are tender, then drain. The addition of two sliced cloves of garlic, 1 tablespoon of dried mint, 1 tablespoon of vinegar and 2 teaspoons of sugar will improve the flavour.

Finish as above.

Mashed Courgette and Tomato Salad

This is a strongly flavoured North African appetizer.

SERVES 6

2 large onions, chopped
4 tablespoons oil
2 cloves garlic, crushed
1 teaspoon ground cumin
1 lb/500 g courgettes, thickly sliced
salt and pepper
2 tablespoons wine vinegar
a good pinch of cayenne (optional)
1 lb/500 g tomatoes, peeled and chopped

Fry the onion in oil until golden. Add the garlic and cumin and stir.

Add the courgettes, salt, pepper, vinegar, cayenne, if used, and the tomatoes.

Put the lid on, and steam in the vegetable juice for about 10 minutes or until the courgettes are very tender.

Mash with a fork or with a potato masher.

Serve cold.

Carrot and Yogurt Salad

HAVUC SALATASI

Serve this refreshing Turkish salad as an appetizer. It is easy to make and looks pretty.

SERVES 6

1 lb/500 g carrots
salt
½ pt/300 ml sheep's milk or strained yogurt
a bunch of parsley, finely chopped
1 lemon, cut into wedges

Peel and cut the carrots into pieces, then boil in slightly salted water until just tender. Drain and mash and stir in the yogurt. Serve sprinkled with parsley and accompanied by lemon wedges.

Celeriac Salad

Turmeric gives this salad a pale yellow tinge and a distinctive flavour.

SERVES 4

2 celeriac, weighing about 2 lb/1 kg
3 cloves garlic, crushed
5 tablespoons olive oil
¼ teaspoon turmeric
salt and pepper
2 teaspoons sugar
juice of 1 lemon

Peel and wash the celeriac and cut into pieces of roughly the same size. Put them in a saucepan with the rest of the ingredients and enough water to cover and cook, uncovered, for 10-20 minutes until soft and the liquid is reduced. Serve cold.

VARIATION

Make this salad with other root vegetables such as potatoes, turnips or swedes.

ROAST PEPPERS IN OLIVE OIL

SALATET FELFEL

When peppers are roasted their flesh becomes deliciously soft and their flavour changes too. But they must be fleshy ones or it is not worth the trouble of peeling them.

This dish is usually made with green peppers only, but it is more attractive with yellow and red ones added.

SERVES 6

6 peppers (green, red and yellow)

4 tablespoons olive oil

salt and pepper

To garnish

a handful of black olives

2 slices of fetta cheese, cubed (optional)

Put the peppers in the hottest part of the oven for about 30 minutes or until they are brown all over, turning them over once.

Put them straight into a polythene bag, close tightly and leave them for about 10 minutes – this makes peeling them easier.

Peel the peppers, pull off the stems, cut them open and remove the seeds – keep their juices. Then cut the softened flesh into largish strips or squares and dress with their juices, the oil, salt and pepper.

Garnish with the olives and, if you like, with pieces of cheese.

VARIATION

For a stronger flavour add 1 tablespoon or more of wine vinegar, 2 crushed cloves of garlic and a good pinch of cayenne to the dressing.

GREEN BEANS IN OLIVE OIL

LOUBIA BI ZEYT

This is a common, everyday Arab salad.

SERVES 4

1 large onion, cut in half and thinly sliced

4 tablespoons olive oil

1 lb/500 g green beans

3 tomatoes, peeled and chopped

salt

1 teaspoon sugar

a few sprigs of parsley, finely chopped

Soften the onion in oil.

Cut the beans in 2 or 3 pieces if they are long. Add the rest of the ingredients, except the parsley, and water to cover, and cook with the lid on for about 15 minutes, or until the beans are tender but still crisp. Add the parsley and remove the lid towards the end to reduce the water. Serve cold.

Beans in Oil

FASULYA PILAKISI

This white bean salad is the most common appetizer in Turkey.

SERVES 6

8 oz/250 g white beans, soaked for at least 1 hour
1 large onion, chopped
¼ pt/150 ml olive oil
2 cloves garlic, sliced
2 sticks of celery with leaves, diced
1 carrot, diced
2 tomatoes, skinned and diced
salt
2 teaspoons sugar

Drain the beans, boil in fresh water for 10 minutes, then simmer for about 30 minutes. Soften the onion in oil, add the garlic and let them both brown slightly. Add the rest of the ingredients, the drained beans and enough water to cover. Cook with the lid on for about 1 hour. Serve cold.

Spinach and Yogurt Salad

BORANI ESFENAJ

A delicate and fresh Iranian salad.

SERVES 4

1 lb/500 g spinach
1 onion, chopped
2 tablespoons oil
2 cloves garlic, crushed
salt and pepper
½ pt/300 ml natural yogurt

Wash the spinach in plenty of water and remove the stems. Drain and squeeze out all the water with your hands.

Fry the onion in oil until golden, add the garlic and when it begins to colour add the spinach, salt and pepper.

Cook, turning the spinach over until it crumples into a soft mass.

Let it cool, then mix with the yogurt in a bowl and chill before serving.

Vegetables with Eggs

SHAKSHOUKA

This Tunisian dish, which has become popular in most countries of the Middle East, can be varied by adding sliced spicy sausages, such as mergez* or chorizos, or courgettes, aubergines and potatoes.

SERVES 4

1 onion, sliced

2 green peppers, deseeded and cut into ribbons

4 tablespoons oil

4 tomatoes, sliced

salt

pepper or a pinch of cayenne (optional)

1 tablespoon chopped mint

4 large eggs

Fry the onion and peppers in oil until they are soft and the onions golden. Add the tomatoes, sprinkle with salt, pepper or cayenne, if used, and mint and break the eggs on top. Cook gently until the eggs have set. Serve with bread.

Tunisian Cauliflower Fritters

SERVES 6

1 large cauliflower

salt

3 oz/75 g plain flour

2 eggs

juice of 1 lemon

4 oz/125 g Gruyère or farmhouse Cheddar, grated

¼ teaspoon ground nutmeg

a good pinch of cayenne (optional)

1 clove garlic, crushed (optional)

oil for deep frying

Boil the cauliflower in slightly salted water for 5 minutes until just tender. Drain and finely chop. Beat the flour with the eggs and lemon juice until well blended. Add the cheese and nutmeg – and, if you like, cayenne and garlic – and stir in the cauliflower. Leave to rest for 30 minutes. Drop by the tablespoonful into hot, but not smoking, oil and deep fry until browned, turning once. Serve hot.

POTATO OMELETTE

MAACOUDA BEL BATATA

This simple but substantial North African omelette makes a good snack meal accompanied by salad. It can be eaten hot or cold, and is an ideal food to take on a picnic.

SERVES 6

1 lb/500 g potatoes
salt
2 large onions
3 tablespoons oil
2 cloves garlic, crushed
6 eggs
bunch of parsley, finely chopped
1½ teaspoons harissa or 1 teaspoon paprika and a good pinch of cayenne*
1 lemon, cut into wedges (optional)

Peel and cut the potatoes into pieces. Boil in salted water until soft, then drain and mash with a fork.

Fry the onions in 2 tablespoons of oil until soft and slightly coloured, add the garlic and when the aroma rises, stir this into the potatoes.

Beat in the eggs, 1 at a time, and add parsley and harissa or paprika and cayenne.

Heat 1 tablespoon of oil in a large frying pan, pour in the egg and potato mixture, and cook over a very low flame for 10-15 minutes until the bottom sets. Then put under the grill for a few minutes until the top is firm and lightly browned.

Serve the omelette hot or cold, accompanied, if you like, by lemon wedges.

SPINACH OMELETTE

EGGAH BEL SABANEH

Almost every kind of vegetable is cooked with eggs, and spinach is especially popular. Many families have this kind of omelette in the refrigerator at all times, ready for an impromptu snack, or to be sent as a packed lunch with the children to school, or with the husband to work. This is an Egyptian version.

SERVES 4

1 medium onion, chopped
2 tablespoons oil
1 lb/500 g spinach
salt and pepper
a pinch of nutmeg
2 tomatoes, peeled and cut into pieces
2 oz/50 g chick-peas, boiled (optional)
4 large eggs

Fry the onion in 2 tablespoons of oil until golden in a large frying pan. Wash the spinach and remove the stems and hard ribs. Squeeze the water out of the leaves with your hands. Shred them or leave them whole, and put them to cook with the onion.

Add salt, pepper, nutmeg and the tomatoes and stir until the spinach crumples. Add the chick-peas (they need soaking for 1 hour and cook in about 1 hour) if you want a more substantial dish.

Beat the eggs lightly with a fork and pour them in. Mix gently and cook, covered, over a very low heat for about 10-15 minutes until they set. Put under the grill to dry the top. Turn out and serve hot or cold. Cut like a cake.

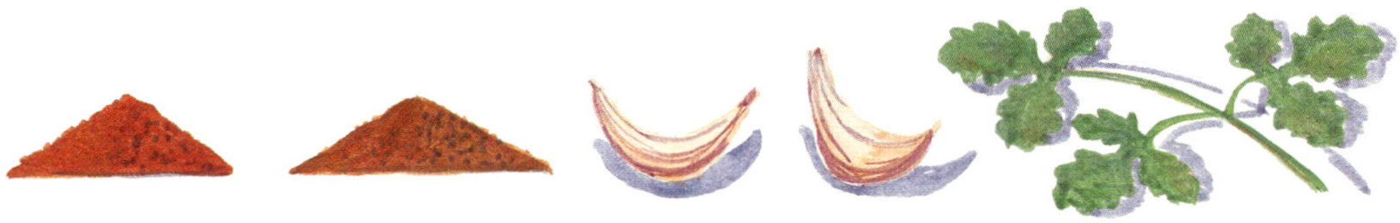

Tunisian Aubergine Tagine

TAGINE BETINJAL

This egg dish takes its name from the earthenware pot it is cooked in. It is good served hot or cold.

SERVES 4

1 lb/500 g aubergines, diced
salt
1 onion, coarsely chopped
oil
2 cloves garlic, crushed
2 oz/50 g Gruyère or Cheddar cheese, grated
1 hard-boiled egg, diced
a bunch of parsley, finely chopped
3 raw eggs, lightly beaten

If you have the time, it is best to sprinkle the aubergines with salt and leave them to drain in a colander for 30 minutes.

Fry the onion in 2 tablespoons of oil until soft. Add more oil, then the aubergines, washed and squeezed gently to get rid of excess water and juices. Fry, stirring, until they are soft and lightly coloured. Add a little more oil if it is soaked up too quickly. Add the garlic and fry, stirring, until the aroma rises. Mix with the rest of the ingredients in a bowl and pour into an oiled shallow ovenproof dish.

Bake in a preheated gas 8/450°F/230°C oven for about 15 minutes or until set.

Stuffed Tomatoes

MAHSHI TAMATEM

Serve as a starter or a light main course.

SERVES 4

4 extra large tomatoes
1 onion, chopped
2 tablespoons oil
8 oz/250 g ground beef
1 tablespoon currants
2 tablespoons walnuts, coarsely chopped
½-1 teaspoon ground cinnamon
½ teaspoon ground allspice
salt and pepper
a small bunch of parsley, finely chopped

Cut a slice off the top of the tomatoes, and scoop out the seeds and some of the pulp.

Fry the onion in oil until it is golden. Add the meat, squash it and stir well until it changes colour. Stir in the currants and walnuts, and add cinnamon, allspice, salt and pepper and parsley. Cook for 8 minutes.

Fill the tomatoes with this mixture and cover with their tops. Put them close to each other in a small baking dish with a little water at the bottom and bake for about 30 minutes at gas 4/350°F/180°C until the tomatoes are soft, but not so soft that they fall apart. Serve hot.

STUFFED PEPPERS

BIBER DOLMASI

This Turkish dish is to be served cold. It is usually made with smallish green peppers, but you can use larger ones and different colours to make a pleasing contrast.

SERVES 6

6 large or 12 small peppers
2 large Spanish onions, finely chopped
¼ pt/150 ml olive oil
2 tablespoons pine nuts
8 oz/250 g short grain rice
2 tablespoons currants
salt and pepper
1 tablespoon sugar
a bunch of mixed parsley, mint and dill, finely chopped

Cut a small slice around the stem end of each pepper and remove the cores and seeds.

To make the filling, fry the onions in 5 tablespoons of oil in a saucepan until golden. Add the pine nuts and when they begin to colour, add the rice, washed and drained, and stir well until it becomes translucent.

Then add the currants, salt, pepper and sugar, and pour in ¾ pt/450 ml water. Let the filling cook with the lid on for 15 minutes, then stir in the herbs.

Pack the filling into the peppers and cover with the tops or, if you prefer, follow the Turkish custom and cover them with slices of tomato.

Place in a baking dish, open side up, and pour in about ¼ pt/150 ml water and the rest of the oil. Cover with a lid or sheet of foil and bake in a preheated gas 5/375°F/190°C oven for 40 minutes. Then uncover and bake for a further 20 minutes until the vegetables are soft. Leave to cool.

VARIATION

Use this filling for other vegetables, such as aubergines, tomatoes or courgettes, to be served cold.

GREEN VEGETABLES

This summer dish of cooked green vegetables – you will find it in Turkey and elsewhere – is as good cold as it is hot.

SERVES 4

1 onion, chopped
3 tablespoons oil
2 cloves garlic, crushed
8 oz/250 g broad beans
2 artichoke hearts, cut in 4 (optional)
salt and pepper
juice of 1 lemon
1 teaspoon sugar
1 lb/500 g spinach or chard

Fry the onion in oil until golden. Add the garlic and, when it begins to colour, add the broad beans and artichoke hearts.

Cover with water, season with salt and pepper, add the lemon juice and sugar, and simmer until the vegetables are only just tender.

In the meantime, wash the spinach or chard and remove stems. Squeeze the water out of the leaves and put them in the pan. Cook for a few minutes longer until the leaves are soft, folding them in as they become limp. Turn into a serving dish.

VARIATIONS

•If the broad beans are very young and tender do not shell them. Leave them in their pods, top and tail them, and cut them in 2 or 3.

•Add 1 lb/500 g Jerusalem artichokes or turnips, cut in 2 or 4, at the same time as the broad beans.

•You may enrich the aromatics with 1 tablespoon of caraway seeds or 1 teaspoon of aniseed and 1 teaspoon of paprika (this will give the dish a North African flavour).

•A bunch of coriander leaves*, coarsely chopped, can be added at the end with the spinach.

•A few tomatoes, peeled, chopped and put in to cook with the greens, add a pleasant note of colour.

Spicy Root Vegetables

This combination of winter vegetables makes a wonderful party dish. The flavouring is Tunisian. The Turks make a similar dish but omit the spices.

SERVES 6

1 celeriac
3 carrots
3 turnips
1 small sweet potato
8 oz/250 g Jerusalem artichokes
5 tablespoons oil
½ teaspoon turmeric
2 teaspoons caraway seeds
salt and pepper
a good pinch of cayenne, or to taste
juice of ½ lemon

Peel and dice all the vegetables and put them in a pan with the rest of the ingredients.

Half cover with water, and cook gently with the lid on for 20 minutes, or until they are done, turning them over so that they are all in the water some of the time (they will also cook in the steam).

Serve hot or cold with their water.

Pumpkin with Raisins and Almonds

This Algerian dish, which sometimes accompanies a simple couscous*, is a fine way of making use of pumpkin.

SERVES 6

3 lb/1.5 kg pumpkin, peeled and cubed
salt and pepper
2 teaspoons ground cinnamon
1 teaspoon sugar
2 tablespoons raisins or sultanas, soaked in water
4 oz/125 g slivered or flaked almonds

Steam the pumpkin for 15-20 minutes or until tender (you can also do this in a pan with a tight-fitting lid and very little water). Mash with a fork, add salt, pepper, cinnamon, sugar (this brings out the flavour of the pumpkin) and stir in the raisins or sultanas. Pour into an oven dish and put under the grill. Toast the almonds under the grill or in a dry frying pan and sprinkle them over the pumpkin before serving.

Sweet and Sour Chard or Spinach Beet Leaves

TERBIYELI DOLMASI

In Turkey, large chard or spinach beet leaves are used like vine leaves and filled with rice. In this dish, their delicate flavour is enhanced by a sweet and sour egg and lemon sauce. You can use large spinach leaves in the same way.

SERVES 6

1 lb/500 g chard or spinach beet leaves

For the filling

1 large onion, coarsely chopped

4 tablespoons light vegetable oil

1 lb/500 g short grain (risotto) rice

1 tablespoon dried mint

juice of ½ lemon

salt

For the sauce

4 eggs

juice of 2 lemons

1-2 tablespoons sugar

salt and pepper

Wash the leaves and cut off the stems, but do not throw them away. Now make the filling. Fry the onion in oil until soft. Add the rice, washed and drained, and the mint, lemon juice and salt. Pour in 2 pt/1.2 litres water, stir well and cook, covered, for about 15 minutes or until the water has been absorbed and the rice is tender.

Then bring plenty of water to the boil in a large pan, plunge in the chard or spinach beet leaves and drain quickly as soon as they are limp. This happens within 1 minute and you must be careful not to overcook or they will break easily.

Line the bottom of a pan with the stems.

Open out each leaf carefully and lay it flat, vein side up. Place 1 tablespoon of the cooled filling at one end (preferably not the stem end) and roll up, folding the two sides in towards the centre when you are midway.

Pack the rolls tightly in layers on top of the stems (these will protect them from burning). Pour 1 pt/600 ml water over them, lay a plate on top and cook very gently for about 30 minutes. Turn out on a serving plate and reserve the cooking liquid.

To make the sauce, beat the eggs and lemon juice with about ¼ pt/150 ml of the cooking liquid and pour into a small saucepan. Add sugar, salt and pepper and stir constantly over low heat until the sauce thickens. Do not let the sauce boil. Pour it over the stuffed leaves and serve cold.

3

FISH

The Mediterranean is not very rich in fish but it offers a great variety. It is all the more curious that not all the countries around the sea make the most of it. I have heard various explanations for this – a chef in Turkey said that in the past people may have thought fish was forbidden by Islam because they did not bleed when they were slit open, and in Morocco I was told that it was because of an ancient fear of the sea and of the things in it.

But there are some really good dishes especially in Turkey and Tunisia, which have the best fish cookery of the region. Many of the dishes are for any kind of fish – at least that's what they say – which makes it easier to find substitutes for those from the Mediterranean.

Red Mullet Grilled in Vine Leaves

SULTAN IBRAHIM

The mullet are impregnated with the flavours of olive oil and garlic, and of the lemony leaves burning over red coals.

SERVES 6

6 small red mullet
4 fl oz/125 ml olive oil
4 cloves garlic, crushed
salt and pepper
a bunch of parsley, finely chopped
12 large vine leaves
1½ lemons, cut in wedges

Scale and gut the fish, but leave the liver inside – it is a delicacy. Prick each one with a needle in a few places.

Beat the olive oil with the garlic, salt, pepper and parsley and marinate the fish in this for 1 hour or longer.

Wrap each fish in 2 vine leaves. Use fresh leaves

as they are or, if using bought ones preserved in salt, desalt them by soaking in a few changes of water for 1 hour.

Grill over a hot charcoal fire, or put the parcels under the grill for about 5-10 minutes, turning them over once. Open a parcel and check that the fish is cooked with a pointed knife. The flesh should have turned from slightly translucent to opaque and almost flaky.

Open out the charred leaves on each individual plate and pass around lemon wedges and what is left of the marinade.

SQUID IN TOMATO SAUCE

MANTIQ TMATIM

Vinegar and saffron make this dish very special.

SERVES 4

2 lb/1 kg squid
1 Spanish onion, chopped
3 tablespoons olive oil
3 cloves garlic, chopped
1 lb/500 g tomatoes, peeled and diced
salt and pepper
1½ tablespoons wine vinegar
½ teaspoon saffron threads (optional)
a bunch of parsley, finely chopped
a bunch of coriander, finely chopped*

Clean the squid, as described on p. 31. Cut the body into rings ½ in/1 cm thick and the tentacles into small pieces.

To make the sauce, fry the onion in oil until soft and golden. Add the garlic and fry until it begins to colour, then add the tomatoes, salt, pepper and vinegar. Crush the saffron, if used, in a spoon with a little water and stir it in.

Put the squid in the sauce, with just enough water to cover. Simmer a few minutes until the squid becomes tender and opaque – this takes 4-5 minutes for baby squid but it can take as long as 45 minutes for a very large one. You must watch the squid constantly, as the flesh hardens quickly if overcooked.

Add the herbs and serve with bread or on a bed of rice.

FISH WITH QUINCE

SAMAK BEL SAFARGAL

I cannot remember how this recipe came to me but it is unusual and delicate and good to serve with couscous* or rice. I like to make it with monkfish.

SERVES 4

2 lb/1 kg monkfish tail
1 in/2.5 cm piece ginger
1 tablespoon tamarind paste*
1 tablespoon sugar
2 cloves garlic, crushed
4 tablespoons olive oil
salt and pepper
1 lb/500 g quince
juice of 1 lemon

Clean the fish. Extract the juice from the ginger by peeling and cutting it into pieces then squeezing it in a garlic press (I picked this method up from a Chinese woman). Put it in a blender with the tamarind, sugar, garlic, oil and a little salt and pepper and rub the fish with the resulting paste.

Peel, core and slice the quince, and drop the slices quickly in a bowl of water with the lemon juice to prevent them from discolouring. Drain and put them at the bottom of a large casserole or frying pan, with just enough water to cover.

Simmer for 10-15 minutes until they are almost done then add the fish with its marinade and cook until it is tender enough for you to cut the spine away with a sharp knife. It will take 8-15 minutes depending on the thickness of the fish. Cut the fish into cubes and heat through. Serve very hot.

Barbecued Prawns

GAMBARI ALA SHISH

Only large fleshy prawns – jumbo or king size – are worth putting on the grill.

SERVES 6

2 lb/1 kg prawns in their shells

For the sauce

6 tablespoons olive oil

3 cloves garlic, crushed

salt

1½ teaspoons ground cumin

1½ teaspoons paprika

a good pinch of cayenne

juice of 1 lemon

Thread the prawns in their shells onto skewers and put them over a charcoal fire or under the grill for about 8 minutes, turning them over once.

Beat the sauce ingredients in a bowl, and serve with the prawns for everyone to dip in.

Fish in Moroccan Sauce

L'HOOTZ BCHERMOULA

Chermoula is the delicious and strongly flavoured sauce – a mixture of herbs and spices with oil – which pervades almost all the fish dishes of Morocco. It varies from town to town and from family to family, but there is always garlic, cumin, paprika, cayenne and fresh coriander*, and often also vinegar or lemon. You can use the sauce as a marinade for almost any fish, and cook it in almost any way – by grilling, frying, baking or steaming.

In Morocco a popular way is to stew the fish very slowly on a bed of vegetables such as potatoes, turnips, broad beans, peppers or tomatoes. But, by the time the vegetables are done, the fish is generally overcooked. I prefer to cook the fish quickly in the marinade and to stew the vegetables separately.

SERVES 4

1½ lb/750 g white fish, such as cod, haddock, hake, coley, whiting or monkfish

5 tablespoons olive oil

3 cloves garlic, crushed

juice of 1 lemon (optional)

salt

1½ teaspoons ground cumin

1 teaspoon paprika

a pinch of cayenne

a bunch of coriander leaves, finely chopped*

Clean, skin and bone the fish, if necessary, and cut it into 1½ in/4 cm cubes. (Monkfish is best cut up when it is cooking and begins to soften.)

Mix the rest of the ingredients, except the lemon, in a bowl. Add 3 tablespoons water, and turn the fish in this marinade. Leave for about 1 hour, covered, in a cool place. Cook the fish for 2-5 minutes (longer for monkfish) in the marinade, turning the pieces over once, until the flesh whitens. Serve hot or cold with lemon juice if you like.

FISH BALLS

COUIRAT EL HOUT

All Middle Eastern countries make some kind of fish balls or fingers which are deep-fried or cooked in sauce. These are Algerian-style and can be served with couscous*.

SERVES 4-6

2 slices of white bread, crusts removed

1½ lb/750 g fillet of cod, haddock, whiting or hake

1 large egg

salt and pepper

a bunch of parsley, finely chopped

For the sauce

1 large onion, finely chopped

3 tablespoons oil

2 cloves garlic, crushed

one 14 oz/400 g can peeled tomatoes

salt and pepper

1 teaspoon paprika

1 teaspoon ground cumin

¼ teaspoon turmeric

a good pinch of cayenne (optional)

juice of ½ lemon, or more

Soak the bread in water and squeeze dry.

Remove any skin and bones from the fish. Chop or mince it and work well with the rest of the ingredients.

A processor will blend to a paste very quickly but be careful not to overblend or the paste will be too soft to handle.

Wet your hands and form little balls the size of a large walnut.

Make the sauce. Fry the onion in oil until golden, add the garlic, and when it begins to colour add the tomatoes and the rest of the ingredients. Pour in ½ pt/300 ml water and bring to the boil.

Drop the fish balls into the sauce and simmer for about 8 minutes, turning them over once.

Serve the fish balls hot or cold in their sauce.

FISH PLAKI

BALIK PILAKISI

Turkish fish plaki is slices of fish cooked with vegetables in a pan and served cold. (The Greek version is a whole fish baked in the oven with fried onions, garlic and tomatoes). It makes a fresh summer meal and a good buffet dish. Fish such as bass, tuna, grey mullet and swordfish are used in Turkey but any kind of white fish – cod, haddock and halibut – will do.

SERVES 4-6

1 large Spanish onion, chopped

5 tablespoons olive oil

2 cloves garlic, crushed

3 medium carrots, diced

½ celeriac (about 8 oz/ 250 g), diced

salt and pepper

1 lemon, cut in slices

1 teaspoon thyme

8 oz/250 g tomatoes, peeled and cut into pieces

2 lb/1 kg fish cut into ¾ in/2 cm slices

a bunch of parsley, chopped

Fry the onion in oil till soft. Add the garlic, carrots and celeriac and stir for about 5 minutes. Pour in ¼ pt/150 ml water, add salt, pepper, lemon and thyme and simmer about 15 minutes or until the vegetables are soft. Add the tomatoes, put in the fish, sprinkle with parsley and simmer gently until the fish is done, making sure that it is bathed in the sauce.

In Turkey they give it 25 minutes but in my view it is better when it has only just turned white and begins to flake when you prick it with a knife. This can take as little as 5 minutes. Let it cool.

FISH COUSCOUS

Do not be alarmed by the number of ingredients – they are there as suggestions to choose from and only need to be thrown into the pot.

This couscous* is Tunisian. The vegetables used are those in season, so choose what you like from those listed (use about half). The fish are those of the Mediterranean, but you can use what you find here such as cod, haddock, halibut and whiting.

SERVES 10 OR MORE

2 lb/1 kg couscous
salt
6 tablespoons oil

For the stew

2 onions, chopped
2 tablespoons oil
4 oz/125 g chick-peas, soaked for 1 hour
½ small cabbage, shredded
4 carrots, quartered
4 turnips, quartered
4 small potatoes, quartered
4 tomatoes, peeled and quartered
4 oz/125 g fresh broad beans
2 peppers, deseeded and shredded
4 courgettes, cut in 4
8 oz/250 g pumpkin, cubed
salt and pepper
1 tablespoon tomato purée
3 lb/1.5 kg fish, cut into large pieces
juice of 1 lemon
a bunch of coriander or parsley, finely chopped*

For the hot sauce

1 tablespoon or more harissa or 1 tablespoon paprika and cayenne to taste*

Prepare the couscous as described on pp. 69-70.

To make the stew fry the onion in oil till golden, add the drained chick-peas, cover with 4 pt/2.4 litres water and simmer for 45 minutes. Put in the vegetables, salt and pepper, tomato purée and more water to cover and cook for another 20 minutes. Add the fish, lemon and herbs and cook for 5-10 minutes (depending on the size of the fish) until it is just done.

To make the hot sauce, pour a few ladlefuls of broth into a bowl and stir in the harissa* or paprika and cayenne to taste.

Serve the grain and the stew separately and pass the sauce around for everyone to help themselves.

FISH STUFFED WITH NUTS

The usual fish for this Tunisian recipe is mullet but I use salmon trout or bass because I like to bone it, and mullet is too difficult to bone.

SERVES 4-6

1 fish weighing 3 lb/1.5 kg
salt and pepper
3 tablespoons oil
juice of ½ lemon

For the filling

2 cloves garlic, crushed
2 tablespoons oil
2 eggs
1 tablespoon lemon juice
6 oz/175 g mixed hazelnuts and walnuts
½-1 fresh chilli, finely chopped
salt and pepper
a bunch of parsley, finely chopped

Scale, gut and wash the fish but leave the head on. Cut open the belly and release the spine and bones from the flesh using your fingers with the help of a sharp pointed knife. Then break the spine near the head and tail and pull it out.

To make the filling, fry the garlic in oil till the aroma rises, add the eggs and lemon off the heat and stir over a very low flame until the eggs set into a light cream then add the rest of the ingredients.

Pack the fish with this and secure the opening with toothpicks. Place on an oiled oven dish, sprinkle with salt and pepper, oil and lemon. Cover with foil and bake in a gas 6/400°F/200°C oven for 30 minutes or until the flesh begins to flake, basting with the juices at least once.

4
MEAT AND POULTRY

Meat and poultry are interchangeable in many dishes, notably stews which are the mainstay of Middle Eastern cooking. Lamb is preferred, but veal and beef are also used. They are cooked long and slowly to melting tenderness with all kinds of pulses, vegetables and fruit. The art lies in marrying the ingredients happily and in flavouring them with delicacy. They are served with rice or couscous* or cracked wheat* or with bread.

Meatballs like stews belong to home cooking while meats grilled on charcoal are part of the restaurant and street vendors' trade. But it is easy to cook kebabs under the grill or on the barbecue. They are fun to make and to eat, and they make an attractive meal accompanied by salads.

SKEWERED CHICKEN PIECES

SHISH TAOUK

A lovely dish; the main thing is not to overcook the chicken, and to keep it moist because it can so easily dry out.

SERVES 4

4 chicken breasts
4 tablespoons olive oil
2-4 cloves garlic, crushed
juice of ½ lemon
pepper
salt
melted butter for basting (optional)

To garnish

1 lemon, cut into wedges
a bunch of parsley, coarsely chopped

Cut the chicken into 1 in/2 cm pieces. Mix the oil, garlic, lemon juice and pepper in a bowl, and leave the chicken pieces in this marinade for 1 hour or longer. Add salt before threading onto skewers (preferably ones with a wide flat blade to prevent the chicken from sliding), and turn over a medium fire

for 6-10 minutes, brushing frequently with the marinade or with melted butter.

Serve at once, straight onto plates or on a serving dish, on a bed of parsley and garnished with lemon wedges.

VARIATIONS

Here are some alternative marinades:

*Instead of garlic use an onion, minced in the blender, and add 1 teaspoon of ground cinnamon. This idea comes from Turkey.

*Joujeh kebab – an Iranian version has a good pinch of saffron, crushed and mixed with the juice of ½ lemon, salt and pepper and 3 tablespoons melted butter.

Here is a recipe I found in Morocco: mix 1 teaspoon paprika and a pinch of cayenne with salt and pepper in 4 tablespoons of olive oil. Serve the dish sprinkled with chopped coriander.

Note: although the breast is the traditional piece to use, meat from the leg is juicier. You may prefer it.

SKEWERED MEATS

SHISH KEBAB

Lamb is the usual meat for kebabs, but beef is also used.

Although it makes for a more attractive presentation to have pieces of tomatoes, onions and peppers interspersed with bay leaves between the cubes of meat, the cooking is more successful if there is only meat on the skewers.

SERVES 6

2 lb/1 kg leg of lamb, or beef (porterhouse, sirloin, fillet or rump steak), cut into 1 in/2 cm cubes

¼ pt/150 ml olive (or other) oil

2 onions, grated

4 bay leaves, crushed

2 tablespoons dried mint or marjoram

pepper

salt

To garnish

2 lemons, cut in wedges

a bunch of parsley or mint

Mix the oil, onions, herbs and pepper in a bowl and soak the meat in this marinade for at least 1 hour or overnight, turning the pieces over once. Lift out the meat, sprinkle with salt and thread on skewers. The most useful skewers are long ones in flattened steel with a sharp point because they prevent the meat from sliding.

Place the filled skewers on an oiled grill about 3 in/7 cm from the embers of a wood or charcoal fire. Cook quickly – 7-10 minutes for lamb, less for beef (it is best rare) – turning over once, so that the outside is well browned while the inside is pink and juicy.

Serve garnished with lemon wedges and sprigs of parsley or mint.

Accompany by a Mixed Arab Salad (p. 26) and warm pitta bread.

KIBBEH IN A TRAY

KIBBEH BIL SANNIEH

This kind of meat pie – with a cracked wheat* and meat paste (this mixture is called kibbeh) for a crust – is a well-known Lebanese and Syrian dish. It is easy to prepare in large quantities.

SERVES 12

Kibbeh mixture for the crust

*1 lb/500 g cracked wheat**

2 lb/1 kg lean tender lamb, preferably from the leg, or minced lamb

1 onion

salt and pepper

1 teaspoon ground cinnamon

1 teaspoon ground allspice

a good pinch of cayenne

5 tablespoons oil to bake the pie

For the filling (hashwa)

1 large onion, finely chopped

2 tablespoons oil

3 tablespoons pine nuts

1 lb/500 g minced beef

salt and pepper

1 teaspoon ground cinnamon

½ teaspoon ground allspice

2 tablespoons currants

First make the crust. Put the cracked wheat in cold water in a bowl for 20 minutes, then rinse in a sieve. (It will have absorbed some water but will still be hard.)

Cut all the fat and gristle away from the lamb.

Put the onion through the food processor, then the meat and seasonings and turn to a paste.

Now blend the cracked wheat with the lamb. To achieve a very soft homogeneous paste, you will have to do it in batches (you may need to add a little cold water by the tablespoonful).

If you do not have a food processor, pound minced lamb with grated onion and cracked wheat, or work it vigorously with your hands.

To prepare the filling, fry the onion in oil until soft, add the pine nuts and fry until golden. Add the meat, seasonings and currants (the currants are an idea from Iraq) and cook, stirring, for about 10 minutes.

Now assemble the pie. Oil a large shallow baking tray about 14 x 16 in/36 x 40 cm. Wet your hands and spread half the kibbeh mixture on the bottom. Spread the filling evenly over it, then cover with the remaining kibbeh mixture, pressing it down.

With a sharp knife, cut deep (but not right through to the bottom), parallel lines ½-1 in/1-2 cm apart, then cross them with diagonal lines to make diamond shapes.

Sprinkle with oil and bake in a preheated gas 6/ 400°F/200°C oven for 45-50 minutes or until brown.

Serve hot or cold (hot is best), accompanied by yogurt and a salad.

Minced Meat on Skewers

KOFTA KEBAB

This is exquisitely aromatic and deliciously soft, but you must be very careful not to dry it out on the fire.

SERVES 6

2 lb/1 kg boneless lamb, preferably from the shoulder

2 onions, grated

salt and pepper

1 teaspoon ground cinnamon

½ teaspoon ground allspice

a pinch of cayenne (optional)

a large bunch of parsley, finely chopped

a few sprigs of mint, finely chopped

To garnish

parsley

1 lemon, cut into wedges

If the meat is lean, add quite a bit of fat to keep it moist and juicy (most of it will melt away). Cut into small pieces, then turn to a paste in the food processor with the rest of the ingredients, (or ask the butcher to mince some for you, and then work it to a soft consistency with your hands). Divide the meat into 6 portions. Wet your hands, take each portion and wrap it around a skewer with a wide flat blade. Shape into a sausage about 5 in/12 cm long and press firmly so that it holds together without sliding on the skewer (it becomes very easy once you have got the feel of it). When all the skewers are filled, place them on an oiled grill and turn over hot embers for 5-8 minutes. Serve at once, straight onto individual plates or on a serving dish, on a bed of parsley and garnished with lemon wedges. Accompany by warm pitta bread and salads.

Note: if you do not have skewers shape the meat into burgers.

VARIATION

A good way of serving this kebab is on a bed of strained ewes' milk or Greek yogurt. Warm up, but do not boil, 3 pt/1.5 litres milk or yogurt. Pour onto the serving plate or onto each individual plate, and place the meat on top. Mix 1 tablespoon paprika with 2 tablespoons of oil and dribble over the dish. Toast or fry 2 tablespoons of pine nuts and sprinkle over the top. Garnish further with chopped parsley.

Meat Balls in Tomato Sauce with Eggs

KEFTA TAGINE

These hot spicy meat balls in tomato sauce, with eggs opened on top, are Moroccan. Serve them as a first or a main course. They are delicious.

SERVES 6

For the sauce

1 ½ large onions, chopped

3 tablespoons oil

2 cloves garlic, crushed

1 ½ lb/750 g tomatoes, peeled and chopped

salt

1 teaspoon ground paprika

½ teaspoon ground cumin

½ teaspoon ground cinnamon

a bunch of parsely, finely chopped

For the meat balls

1 ½ lb/750 g minced lamb or veal

a small bunch of parsley, finely chopped

a small bunch of coriander, finely chopped*

a few mint leaves or 2 teaspoons dried mint

salt

1 teaspoon ground paprika

1 teaspoon ground cumin

1 teaspoon ground cinnamon

¼ teaspoon ground ginger

To finish

6 eggs

You will need a wide flameproof pot or casserole which you can take to the table.

Prepare the sauce. Fry the onions in oil until golden, add the garlic and when the aroma rises add the rest of the ingredients. Add ½ pt/300 ml water and simmer for 15 minutes.

In the meantime, make the meat balls. Mix all the ingredients together and work them to a paste with your hands.

Wet your hands and roll them into marble-sized balls, drop them into the sauce and simmer for 15 minutes.

About 10 minutes before you are ready to serve, break open the eggs over the simmering stew. They will stay on the surface and the dish will be ready when they are set. Do not let them become too firm.

Meat Balls with Okra

KOFTA BI BAMIA

SERVES 4

1 lb/500 g okra

1 lb/500 g minced lamb

salt and pepper

1 teaspoon ground cinnamon

¼ teaspoon ground allspice

2 tablespoons parsley, chopped

1 large onion, thinly sliced

3 tablespoons oil

1 clove garlic, sliced

3 large tomatoes, peeled and cut into pieces

juice of ½ lemon (optional)

Wash the okra and trim the stems but do not cut through the pod or the gelatinous juice will come out in the cooking.

Make the meat balls. Mix the meat, salt, pepper, cinnamon, allspice and parsley and work well with your hands into a soft paste. Roll into small balls the size of a large hazelnut.

Fry the onion in oil until soft. Add the garlic and the meat balls and fry, shaking the pan and turning the meat balls so as to colour them all over.

Then add the okra and tomatoes, a little salt and pepper and enough water just to cover.

Simmer, with the lid on, for about 25 minutes or until the okra are tender. Stir in the lemon juice if used.

Serve hot with rice or with cracked wheat*.

Courgettes Stuffed with Meat in Apricot Sauce

MAHSHI COUSA BI MISHMISH

For this dish you can use small courgettes or larger ones cut in half. Smaller ones are more elegant, but they must be thick enough to allow an apple corer – the long, thin kind – through their centre. Serve hot with rice.

SERVES 6-12

12 courgettes about 5 in/ 12 cm long

For the filling

1 large Spanish onion, finely chopped

2 tablespoons oil

3 tablespoons pine nuts

1 lb/500 g minced lamb, beef or veal

salt and pepper

1 teaspoon ground cinnamon

¼ teaspoon allspice

For the sauce

2 cloves garlic

2 tablespoons oil

1 lb/500 g tomatoes, peeled and chopped

1 tablespoon dried mint

juice of 1½-2 lemons

8 oz/250 g dried apricots (the sharp dark variety), chopped

Wash the courgettes and slice off the stem end. Using a thin, long apple corer, make a hole through the stem end of each courgette and scoop out the pulp by burrowing in and giving a sharp twist before reaching the end. (It will seem difficult until you get the knack of it.) Be careful not to break the skin.

To make the meat filling, fry the onion in 2 tablespoons of oil until golden. Add the pine nuts and fry until lightly coloured. Then add the meat and fry, stirring and crushing it with a fork, until it changes colour. Add salt, pepper, cinnamon and allspice.

When the filling has cooled a little, pack it into the courgettes and arrange them side by side in a shallow ovenproof dish.

Now make the apricot sauce. Fry the garlic in 2 tablespoons of oil, and when the aroma rises add the rest of the ingredients. Cover with water, cook 10 minutes and pour this sauce over the courgettes. Add more water, if necessary, to half cover the courgettes and bake in a gas 5/375°F/190°C oven for 30 minutes or until they are tender.

Chicken Tagine with Onions and Tomatoes

DJEJ MATISHA MESLA

In this Moroccan dish, the chicken cooks in the juice of fresh tomatoes and onions and is sweetened at the end with honey.

SERVES 4

4 chicken quarters

3 tablespoons oil

3 onions, grated

2 lb/1 kg tomatoes, peeled and cut into pieces

salt and pepper

¼ teaspoon ground ginger

2 teaspoons ground cinnamon

½ teaspoon saffron powder (optional)

2 tablespoons honey

2 tablespoons sesame seeds (optional)

Put all the ingredients, except the honey and sesame seeds, in a large pan and cook gently, covered, turning the chicken pieces over occasionally, until the flesh is so tender it can be pulled off the bone easily.

Remove the chicken, and reduce the sauce to a thick sizzling cream. Stir as it begins to caramelize and be careful that it does not stick or burn. Stir in the honey, return the chicken pieces to the sauce and heat through.

Serve the chicken covered with the sauce and, if you like, sprinkled with sesame seeds toasted under the grill.

LAMB IN YOGURT SAUCE

LABAN IMMO

This is an Arab dish. The name literally means 'his mother's milk', the image being that of a young lamb cooked in yogurt made from ewes' milk. Serve with rice or cracked wheat*.

SERVES 6

1½ lb/750 g lean tender lamb, cut from the leg or fillet and cubed

8 oz/250 g small pickling onions

salt and pepper

1 cinnamon stick

1½ pt/900 ml sheep's milk or strained yogurt

2 tablespoons cornflour

1 tablespoon dried mint

2 cloves garlic, crushed (optional)

Put the meat in a pan with just enough water to cover. Bring to the boil and remove the scum. Add the onions, salt, pepper and cinnamon, and simmer for about 45 minutes until the meat is tender, adding water so as to have a good amount of sauce.

Heat up the yogurt in another pan. Before it gets too hot, mix the cornflour with a few tablespoons of water in a cup and pour it in. This will 'stabilize' the yogurt and prevent it from curdling, and also serves to thicken the sauce. Stir constantly (you are supposed to do this always in the same direction, but I don't know why) as the yogurt comes to the boil slowly and begins to thicken.

Add mint, and garlic if used, stir well, and pour over the meat. Cook gently for about 10 minutes longer.

VARIATIONS

*Fresh broad beans can be thrown in 15 minutes before adding the yogurt.

*A beautiful dish is made with the addition of stuffed courgettes (p. 61). Put them into the stew from the start.

VEAL TAGINE WITH JERUSALEM ARTICHOKES

M'QUALI

This is a Moroccan stew. The name 'tagine' comes from the shallow clay baking dish in which it is put to cook straight onto a charcoal fire. Saffron gives it a more delicate flavour, but turmeric (also called oriental saffron) is what is used by street vendors. You cannot get the Moroccan preserved olives which are used for cooking here, but the Greek calamatas and Italian agaetas are good alternatives.

SERVES 6

1½ lb/750 g stewing veal
1 onion, finely chopped
1 clove garlic, finely chopped
salt and pepper
¼ teaspoon ground ginger
½ teaspoon saffron powder or turmeric
1½ lb/750 g Jerusalem artichokes
1 preserved lemon, chopped up or juice of 1 lemon*
a handful of olives (optional)
a bunch of coriander, finely chopped*

Put the meat in a heavy pan with the onion and garlic, cover with water, bring to the boil and remove any scum. Add salt, pepper and spices and cook, covered, for about 1 hour or until the meat is very tender. Peel the artichokes and cut them in pieces, if they are large. Then add the rest of the ingredients and cook for 15 minutes. Be careful not to overcook the artichokes as they fall apart very quickly.

VARIATIONS

*Use potatoes, turnips or sweet potatoes instead of Jerusalem artichokes.

*You can add a handful of currants.

*You can also add 2 or 3 tomatoes, peeled and chopped.

LAMB WITH AUBERGINES AND DATES

SIKBAJ

A mixture of puréed dates and vinegar (a combination that has come down from ancient Persia to the countries of North Africa) gives a wonderful sweet and sour flavour to this aromatic stew. It is very easy to make in large quantities.

SERVES 6-8

1½ lb/750 g aubergines, cubed
2 large onions, cut in half then sliced
3 tablespoons oil
1½ lb/750 g lean lamb, cubed
salt and pepper
1 teaspoon ground cinnamon
½ teaspoon ground allspice
¼ teaspoon ground ginger
6 oz/175 g dried dates
4-5 tablespoons wine vinegar
*2 tablespoons rose water**
4 oz/125 g blanched almonds

Sprinkle the aubergines with salt, let them degorge their juices in a colander for 30 minutes, then rinse the salt off.

Fry the onions in oil until golden. Add the meat and turn to brown it all over.

Add the pepper, cinnamon, allspice and ginger and cover with water. Bring to the boil, remove any scum, then simmer for 1 hour or until the meat is tender. Add the aubergines and cook for 30 minutes longer.

Stone the dates and put them with the vinegar and a little water (enough to have a thick cream) in the blender. Pour this sauce over the stew. Sprinkle with rose water and cook for a few minutes longer.

Serve hot, garnished with the almonds heated in a dry frying pan.

Beef with Broad Beans and Spinach

LAHMA BI FOUL AHDAR WA SABANEKH

This Egyptian stew can be served with rice or cracked wheat*. The dried limes* introduce an Iraqi flavour.

SERVES 4-6

1 onion, chopped
3 tablespoons oil
2 cloves garlic, crushed
1 lb/500 g beef, cubed
salt and pepper
*2 dried limes**
2 lb/1 kg broad beans
1 lb/500 g spinach

Fry the onion in oil until golden. Add the garlic and meat and turn to brown it all over. Sprinkle with salt and pepper, add the limes, cover with water and simmer, covered, for 45 minutes-1 hour or until tender. Add water if necessary. Cut the limes open when they are soft.

Take the beans out of their pods, drop them in and cook for 10 minutes longer. Wash the spinach thoroughly and remove the stems. Stir in the leaves and cook for a few minutes more, then serve.

Meat and Prune Stew

KHORESH ALOU

This fruity Iranian stew is rich in green herbs and has the special mellow flavour of dried limes*. Serve it hot with plain rice.

SERVES 6

2 onions chopped
1½ lb/750 g stewing lamb or beef, cubed
salt and pepper
2 dried limes
8 oz/250 g pitted prunes
1 lb/500 g spinach
a bunch of spring onions, finely chopped

Fry the onions in oil until golden then add the meat and brown it all over. Season with salt and pepper, add the limes, cover with water and simmer very gently for 1½ hours or until the meat is tender, adding more water as necessary. As soon as the limes are soft enough, pierce them with the point of a knife so that they can give more of their flavour.

Add the prunes, spinach (stems removed, washed and shredded) and spring onions and cook for 30 minutes longer. Serve at once.

LAMB AND CELERIAC STEW

TERBIYELI KEREVIZ

A delicate Turkish stew with an egg and lemon sauce.

SERVES 4

2 celeriac, weighing about 2½ lb/1.25 kg

2 onions, cut in half and sliced thinly

3 tablespoons oil

1 lb/500 g lean fillet or leg of lamb, cut in pieces

salt and pepper

For the sauce

2 egg yolks

juice of ½ lemon

Peel the celeriac and cut each one into quarters.

Fry the onions in oil until soft. Add the meat and let it brown all over. Add the celeriac, salt and pepper, and cover with water.

Simmer, covered, for about 1 hour or until the meat is very tender. As soon as the celeriac is tender enough, lift it out and cut it into sticks.

When the meat is done, put the celeriac back into the pan to cook for a few minutes longer until it is soft.

Make the sauce just before you are ready to serve. Beat the egg yolks with the lemon juice and a few tablespoons of liquid from the stew and pour this back into the pan. Stir for a minute or so until the sauce thickens, but do not let it boil. Serve hot.

SWEETBREADS

HALAWAYAAT

Sweetbreads have a great delicacy of flavour and texture and are far easier to use than the French lead you to believe. You can generally find them frozen.

SERVES 6

2 lb/1 kg veal or lamb sweetbreads

salt and white pepper

1 teaspoon ground cinnamon

½ teaspoon ground cardamom

1 teaspoon paprika

2 oz/50 g butter

1 tablespoon oil

juice of 1 lemon

a small bunch of parsley, finely chopped

Put the sweetbreads into cold water, bring to the boil and simmer for 5 minutes, then refresh under cold water and drain.

Remove the gelatinous membranes and any fatty or horny bits carefully from veal sweetbreads, then cut into walnut-sized pieces. Remove any hard bits from lamb sweetbreads.

Season with salt and pepper, and sprinkle with cinnamon, cardamom and paprika. Heat the butter and oil in a frying pan, and when it begins to sizzle put in the sweetbreads and let them cook for 6 minutes until they turn pale golden. Add the lemon juice and serve garnished with parsley.

Lamb Stew with Apricots

MISHMISHEYA

Sugar is usually added as well as a handful of raisins to this delicate cinnamon flavoured Tunisian dish, but I have left them out as the apricots are sweet enough.

It is easy to make in large quantities for a party and you can make it long in advance and reheat it gently.

SERVES 8

2 onions, cut in half then sliced
3 tablespoons oil
2 lb/1 kg lamb (shoulder or fillet) trimmed of fat and cubed
8 oz/250 g chick-peas, soaked for 1 hour
pepper
3 teaspoons ground cinnamon
salt
1½ lb/750 g fresh apricots, pitted and cut in half

Fry the onion in oil until golden. Add the meat and turn to brown it all over. Add the drained chick-peas, cover with water and bring to the boil. Remove any scum, add pepper and cinnamon and simmer for an hour or longer until the meat and chick-peas are very tender. Do not add salt until the chick-peas have begun to soften.

Add the apricots and cook for a further 20 minutes. They should be really soft. Serve the stew with plain rice or couscous*.

Quails with Cracked Wheat

SIMAN BIL BURGHUL

In this Egyptian dish the quails are usually stuffed with cracked wheat*, but it is better and simpler to cook them separately.

SERVES 4

8 quails
2 onions, finely chopped or grated
4 tablespoons oil
salt and pepper
2 cardamom pods, cracked open
1 teaspoon cinnamon
1 teaspoon cumin
1 teaspoon coriander

For the stuffing

*1 lb/500 g coarse cracked wheat**
2 pt/1.2 litres stock or water
salt and pepper
3 tablespoons oil or butter
4 tablespoons currants
4 oz/125 g shelled walnuts, chopped

Make the stuffing first. Put the cracked wheat in a pan with the stock or water. Add salt and pepper, the oil or butter and the currants. Bring to the boil, and simmer, covered, for 20 minutes. Then stir in the walnuts and let it rest, still covered, off the heat for 10 minutes, until the grain is plump and tender.

Clean the quails, soften the onions in oil and put the birds in. Add the salt and spices and sauté the quails quickly, turning to brown all over. Put the lid on and cook for about 10 minutes or until they are done. Serve the quails buried in the cracked wheat.

Chicken with Lemon and Olives

DJEJ MQUALI

The flavour of lemons which have lost their sharpness through preservation in salt belongs to Morocco where it pervades many cooked dishes and salads. At every vegetable market you can see stalls laden with huge piles of soft lemons oozing with juice beside several varieties of olives. The two are often used together, as they are in this dish. Instructions for making your own preserved lemons (it is very easy) are given on p. 89 and the nearest you can get to Moroccan preserved olives are Italian agaetas and Greek calamatas.

SERVES 4

1 chicken, with giblets

1 large onion, coarsely chopped

2 tablespoons olive or vegetable oil

1 clove garlic, crushed

¼ teaspoon ground ginger

¼ teaspoon saffron coloured powder

a pinch of real saffron threads (optional)

salt

the chicken liver

1-2 preserved lemons

2-3 oz/50-75 g Moroccan red olives, Italian agaetas or Greek calamatas

In Morocco a chicken dish is more highly esteemed if the bird comes to the table whole, but when its excellence depends on long slow cooking in flavoursome juices it makes more sense to cut it up into pieces and to have them soaking in the sauce.

Fry the onions in oil in a large heavy saucepan. Add garlic, ginger, the 2 saffrons (the real thing is for flavour, the powder for colour) and pour in ¼ pt/150 ml water.

Put in the chicken pieces and the liver and cook very gently, covered, turning the chicken over frequently and adding a little water if necessary, until the chicken is so tender that the flesh comes off the bone when you pull it.

Lift out the chicken pieces. Mash the liver or put it through the blender with some of the onions, then return it to the pan (it is meant to enrich the sauce). Reduce the sauce further if necessary until it has a rich thick consistency.

Add the preserved lemon peels washed and chopped up, and the olives – first soaked in water for 15 minutes then boiled in fresh water for another two.

Put the chicken back into the saucepan to heat it through.

Serve with the sauce, lemons and olives poured on top.

VARIATION

An Algerian version which you might like to try has 2 or 3 tomatoes, peeled and chopped, put in at the start and a bunch of fresh coriander*, coarsely chopped, towards the end.

Quails with Grapes

SOUMANAT BIL EINAB

This is a Moroccan dish.

SERVES 4

4 quails
2 tablespoons butter
1 tablespoon oil
1 teaspoon ground cinnamon
salt and pepper
1½ in/3 cm piece fresh ginger root
8 oz/250 g grapes, deseeded

Clean the quails. Sauté very quickly in a mixture of butter and oil, adding salt, pepper, cinnamon and the juice extracted from the ginger (see p. 50). (In Morocco dried ginger powder is used, but the juice gives a fresher taste.) Turn the quails to brown them all over.

Add the grapes and cook, covered, for 10 minutes, turning the quails once more.

Serve hot.

Couscous with Vegetables

Couscous*, a kind of semolina, is a staple food and the national dish of the countries of North Africa. The name also applies to the stew or garnish that goes with it.

There are many versions. This Moroccan one consists of a delicately spiced stew made with chicken, lamb or veal and a lot of fresh vegetables. The grain is then prepared separately (using the pre-cooked packet variety sold here, this is extremely easy).

It is a meal in itself and worth making for a large party – a matter of putting things in the pot at different times.

The shoulder of lamb, which is commonly used, needs to be boned and to have the fat removed. The fillet is easier, and you can also use a knuckle of veal or stewing beef, or a mixture of meats. For the vegetables, make a large selection (the usual number is 7).

If you want to vary the presentation, or make it hot as they do in Tunisia and Algeria, look at the variations at the end of the recipe.

SERVES 10 OR MORE

2 lb/1 kg couscous
salt
6 tablespoons oil

For the stew

4-6 chicken pieces and/or 2 lb/1 kg meat
2 lb/1 kg onions
salt and pepper
½ teaspoon saffron powder
1 tablespoon paprika
1 small white cabbage, cut into large pieces
1 lb/500 g carrots, cut in half lengthways
4 oz/125 g fresh broad beans
8 oz/250 g turnips, cut in half or quartered
1 medium aubergine, cubed
3 small chillies, finely chopped
8 oz/250 g courgettes, sliced in 4
8 oz/250 g pumpkin
1 lb/500 g tomatoes, peeled and quartered
a very large bunch of coriander, finely chopped*

First make the stew. Put the chicken and/or meats into a large pan with plenty of water, bring to the boil and remove the scum. Add 2 finely chopped onions, salt, pepper, saffron, paprika and the cabbage, and simmer, covered, for about 1 hour.

Put in the remaining onions (quartered), the carrots, broad beans, turnips, aubergine and chillies, with more water to cover, and simmer for 30 minutes longer. The meat should be tender.

Then add the rest of the ingredients, check the seasoning and cook 20-30 minutes more.

In the meantime, prepare the grain in a large bowl. Moisten with a little less than its volume of salted water (less than 1¾ pt/1 litre). Add the water gradually and stir well so that it becomes absorbed evenly. Rub the grain between your palms to fluff it up and remove any lumps. After about 10 minutes, when it is plump and tender, add the oil (butter is the usual fat but oil makes it lighter) and steam it over the stew or over boiling water to heat it through (it does not need cooking). It is ready just as soon as you can see steam come out of the top. It will become soggy if it is left too long. The steaming is traditionally done in the top part of a couscousière (see p. 12).

Alternatively, you can more easily heat up the moistened grain in a saucepan or in the oven (in a pot with a lid). There is nothing easier.

To serve, turn the couscous out in a large round dish. Make a well in the centre of the mound. With a slotted spoon, lift out the meats and vegetables and place them in the well.

Serve the broth separately.

VARIATIONS

*Add 6 oz/175 g chick-peas (soaked for at least 1 hour) at the start.

*For another presentation, serve the stew in a separate bowl. Shape the couscous in a pointed cone and garnish with 4 oz/125 g raisins or sultanas, simmered first for 10 minutes in a little water, and with 4 oz/125 g toasted almonds. Draw lines like rays coming down from the point with a dusting of cinnamon.

To make a hot Tunisian-style sauce, take a few ladlefuls of broth and stir in 1 or 2 tablespoons of harissa, or the same amount of paprika and a good pinch of cayenne. Omit the saffron (it would be wasted) and add 2 teaspoons ground allspice. Pass the sauce around in a bowl for everyone to help themselves.

MEAT AND VEGETABLE POT

TURLUSU

This rich Turkish summer stew is a meal in itself served with rice or cracked wheat*. There are no herbs or spices. All the flavour comes from the vegetables.

SERVES 6

2 medium onions
2 tablespoons oil
1 lb/500 g tender lamb or beef, cubed
salt and pepper
1 medium aubergine, cubed
4 oz/125 g okra, trimmed
2 green or red peppers, deseeded and cut into ribbons
8 oz/250 g green beans, strings removed
3 tomatoes, skinned and quartered
2 courgettes, sliced thick

Fry the onions in oil.

Add the meat and brown it all over, then cover with water, sprinkle with salt and pepper and simmer for about 40 minutes.

Add the vegetables – put in the tomatoes and courgettes when the rest are almost tender – and cook for another 30 minutes until done to your liking. (In Turkey the vegetables are cooked until they are very soft, but you may prefer them to be crisp.)

VARIATION

For a winter pot use potatoes, celeriac, leeks and carrots instead of the summer vegetables.

Rabbit with Vinegar

ARNAB MUKHALAL

In the Muslim world where alcohol is forbidden, vinegar is used in cooking where wine would be used in other countries. It gives this dish a rich, strong flavour. But start with the smaller quantity and add more later to taste.

SERVES 4

1 rabbit cut into pieces
3-4 tablespoons oil
1 lb/500 g small pickling onions, whole or 2 large ones, coarsely chopped
1 clove of garlic, crushed
1 lb/500 g tomatoes, peeled and chopped
3-5 fl oz/75-150 ml red wine vinegar
salt and pepper
½ teaspoon ground allspice
1 teaspoon ground cinnamon
1 cardamom pod, cracked
1 tablespoon sugar
2-3 tablespoons currants
small bunch of parsley, finely chopped

Brown the rabbit pieces in the oil in a large casserole. Take them out and fry the onions in the same oil until golden, then add the garlic.

Put the rabbit pieces back into the pot with the tomatoes. Pour in the vinegar and add salt, pepper, allspice, cinnamon, cardamom and sugar. Add enough water to cover the rabbit.

Cover with the lid and simmer for about 1½ hours, or until the rabbit is very tender.

Add the currants and parsley towards the end and stir through. Remove the lid and continue cooking to reduce the sauce until it is thick and creamy.

Serve with plain rice or cracked wheat*.

Note: you may also cook the rabbit in the oven preheated to gas 4/350°F/180°C. It will take about 2 hours.

CHICKEN WITH COUSCOUS STUFFING

Usually this chicken is stuffed with steamed couscous* and then cooked in a spicy sauce, but it is easier, and just as good, to cook and serve the stuffing separately. It is a sweet dish with a fair amount of sugar, which you may prefer to reduce, or omit altogether, but keep the honey in the sauce.

SERVES 4

one 3 lb/1.5 kg chicken
1 onion, grated or finely chopped
3 tablespoons oil
1 teaspoon ground cinnamon
¼ teaspoon ground ginger
¼ teaspoon saffron powder
salt and pepper
2 cloves garlic, crushed
2 tablespoons icing sugar (optional)
2 tablespoons honey

For the stuffing

*1 lb/500 g packet couscous**
salt
1-2 tablespoons caster sugar (optional)
4 tablespoons oil
3 oz/75 g raisins, soaked in water for a few minutes
*2 tablespoons orange flower water**
8 oz/250 g blanched almonds
2 oz/50 g shelled pistachios

Clean the chicken. Soften the onion in oil in a large pan. Add the spices, salt, pepper and garlic and put in the chicken.

Add ½ pt/300 ml water and simmer, covered, for about 1 hour or until the chicken is tender, turning it over occasionally so that it is well impregnated with the sauce.

In the meantime, make the stuffing. Put the couscous in a bowl with ¾ pt/450 ml water and a little salt. Stir well and let it absorb the water for 10-15 minutes, then rub with your hands to break up any soggy lumps. Add sugar, if used, 3 tablespoons oil, raisins and orange flower water, and stir in with your hands. Fry the almonds and pistachios in the remaining oil, chop them coarsely then stir them into the couscous. It now only needs to heat through in a pan; add a little water, if it is not quite tender, and put the lid on.

Take the chicken out, cover it with 2 tablespoons icing sugar and put it in a very hot oven to caramelize for 15-20 minutes. If you omit this step you may need to cook the chicken longer in the pan.

Boil the chicken sauce to reduce it and add 2 tablespoons of honey.

To serve, put the chicken in the middle of a large round dish. Put a ring of hot stuffing around it and pour the sauce on top.

Poussins with Rice

ROZ OU JAJ

There are a great many chicken and rice recipes in Arab cooking. In this Egyptian dish, baby chickens are braised with spices, and the rice is cooked in stock (made here with chicken wings) and garnished with nuts and chicken livers. It is a long recipe, but it does not take long to cook and it constitutes a party meal.

SERVES 4-8

4 poussins (spring chickens)

3 tablespoons oil

2 cloves garlic, crushed

salt and pepper

1 teaspoon ground cinnamon

½ teaspoon ground allspice

½ teaspoon ground cardamom

½ teaspoon ground cumin

For the rice

8 chicken wings

1 onion, cut into 4

salt and pepper

2 cardamom pods

1 lb/500 g long grain rice

3 tablespoons oil

8 oz/250 g nuts, such as slivered almonds, chopped hazelnuts, pistachios and pine nuts

For the garnish

1 large onion, finely chopped

3 tablespoons oil

3 tablespoons raisins or currants

8 oz/250 g chicken livers

salt and pepper

½ teaspoon ground allspice

1 teaspoon ground cinnamon

Make the stock for the rice. Simmer the wings with the onion, salt, pepper and cardamom pods in 2 pt/1.2 litres water for at least 1 hour, removing any scum at the beginning.

Wash the poussins. Put the oil, garlic, salt and spices in a large pan with ½ pt/300 ml water, bring them to the boil and put in the chickens. Simmer very gently, covered, for about 30 minutes or until the birds are tender, turning them over a few times and adding water as it becomes absorbed.

Alternatively, you can bake the birds in the oven. Rub them with oil and a mixture of the spices and put them in a casserole, breast down. Put the lid on and bake in a gas 7/425°F/220°C oven for 20-30 minutes or until done.

Wash and drain the rice, and stir it in 2 tablespoons of oil on a very low heat for 1-2 minutes until it becomes translucent. Add the strained stock. Bring to the boil, then cook, covered, on a very low heat for about 20 minutes until the rice is tender, adding a little water if it is absorbed too quickly.

Skin and bone the wings, and cut the flesh up small. Fry the nuts in 1 tablespoon of oil until the almonds are slightly coloured, and stir both into the rice.

For the garnish, fry the onion in oil until soft, add the raisins or currants, the trimmed chicken livers, seasoning and spices. Fry very quickly (1-2 minutes) on high heat, shaking the pan until the livers are well browned but still pink inside.

To serve, shape the rice in a mound with the livers on top and the chickens round it. Everything must be very hot.

5

GRAINS, PASTA & PULSES

Apart from North Africa where couscous* (a kind of semolina of Berber origin) is the staple food, a bowl of rice comes with the main meal in most Middle Eastern cities. In the countryside, wheat, either cracked or whole, pasta or beans (brown in Egypt, white in Turkey) take its place.

All of these are embellished with herbs and spices, with garnishes and by mixing with all kinds of other ingredients.

PLAIN RICE

ROZ

There are different kinds of rice in the Middle East ranging from long grain and round (which is used for fillings and for puddings) to the very thin grain of Iran and Iraq. Every country has its own special way of cooking it and each requires a different quantity of water. This is one of the simplest ways.

SERVES 4-6

1 lb/500 g long grain rice
3 tablespoons oil
salt

Soak the rice in salted water for at least an hour. This gets rid of the fine powder which makes it sticky.

Heat the oil in a heavy bottomed or non-stick saucepan. Throw in the well drained rice and stir until it becomes transparent (this helps to keep it separate). Pour in 1¼ pt/750 ml water and stir in a little salt. Bring to the boil, then cook, covered, on the lowest possible heat for about 20 minutes. If you use a non-stick pan you can turn it out like a cake.

BASMATI STEAMED RICE

The best quality long grain rice you can buy here is basmati which is small and thin and comes from India and Pakistan. It remains firm and separate when cooked and has an enchanting flavour and aroma. My favourite way of cooking it – partially boiled and then left to steam in the saucepan – is inspired by, but less perfectionist than the Iranian way. It is very easy and once you will have got used to it you will never fail to make perfect rice.

SERVES 4-6

1 lb/500 g basmati rice
salt
4 tablespoons butter

Wash the rice in a colander (this removes the starchy powder which makes it sticky) then put it in a bowl of lukewarm water with 1 tablespoon of salt (it does not penetrate the rice but helps to keep it separate) and leave it to soak for 1 hour or longer.

Bring plenty of water to boil in a saucepan with 2 tablespoons of salt (it still does not make the rice salty). Drain the rice, sprinkle it in and let it boil vigorously for between 4-6 minutes. Take a grain and test it – it must be still a little hard. Drain quickly.

Put 2 tablespoons of butter at the bottom of the empty pan, put the rice on top, add 2 more tablespoons of butter and stir well. Put the pan on the lowest possible heat with the lid on and let it steam for 20-30 minutes. Serve hot.

Note: you can use oil instead of butter.

IRANIAN JEWEL ENCRUSTED RICE

DJAVAR POLO

The 'jewels' in this beautiful chicken and rice dish are a multicoloured assortment of nuts and bits of carrot. When candied orange peel is added the dish is called 'shirin (sweet) polo'. Make it for special occasions as it takes some time to prepare.

SERVES 6-8

1 chicken, weighing 3½-4 lb/1½-2 kg
salt and pepper
2 tablespoons oil
peel of 2 oranges (optional)
4 tablespoons sugar (optional)
4 tablespoons butter
3 large carrots, coarsely grated
1 teaspoon ground cinnamon
2 tablespoons raisins
2 tablespoons currants
¼ teaspoon saffron threads (optional)
4 tablespoons slivered almonds
4 tablespoons pistachios cut in half lengthways
1 lb/500 g long grain rice, soaked in salted water for at least 1 hour

A good way to cook the chicken so that it is tender and juicy is to wrap it in foil. Lay it on a large sheet, sprinkle with salt, pepper and oil and rub them in with your hands. Wrap the chicken up and bake in a gas 4/350°F/180°C oven for 1½ hours or until it is very tender and the juices which come out of a thigh when it is pricked with a fork are no longer pink.

If you want to make it a sweet (shirin) polo, use bought candied orange peel and cut it into thin strips or make your own: remove only the orange part of the rind and leave the white part which is bitter. Cut it into strips or chop it up in a food processor then blanch it twice in clean water each time to remove the bitterness. Add sugar, cover with water and simmer until the syrup thickens (be careful that it does not caramelize and become hard).

Prepare the carrots. Melt 2 tablespoons of butter with 1 tablespoon of oil in a large frying pan, add the carrot with a little salt and cinnamon and sauté, stirring often, for about 10 minutes until they are soft. Add the orange peel if you are using it, the raisins, currants and saffron, if you like (crushed in a spoon and mixed with a tablespoon of water). Cook for 5 minutes, then add the almonds and pistachios.

Sprinkle the drained rice into boiling salted water and let it boil vigorously for 4-8 minutes until it is almost tender (bite a grain – it should still be a little hard). Watch that it does not become soft (it can do so very suddenly). Drain quickly then return the rice to the pan. Add 2 tablespoons of butter and stir in ⅔ of the carrot and nut mixture. Put the pan on a very low heat with the lid on and let it steam for 20 minutes or until the rice is tender.

When you are ready to serve, skin and bone the chicken and cut it into pieces. Pour half the rice mixture on a large flat serving plate, spread the chicken pieces on top and cover with the rest of the rice. Pour the chicken juices all over and garnish with the remaining carrot and nut mixture. Everything must be very hot.

VARIATION

This recipe can be made with meat balls instead of chicken. Work 1¼ lb/625 g minced lamb with a small grated onion, salt and pepper and ½ teaspoon ground cinnamon and roll into marble-sized balls. Fry in a little oil for 8-10 minutes shaking the pan to brown them all over. Arrange them between two layers of rice.

CRACKED WHEAT

BURGHUL

Cracked wheat* is the staple of Turkey and the part of the Arab world which was called the Fertile Crescent. It is nourishing and very easy to prepare. Many recipes for burghul pilaf combine it with meat or chicken and other ingredients. This one is the simplest. Use it to accompany any of the main dishes and as an alternative to rice.

SERVES 4

1 lb/500 g cracked wheat
salt
2 tablespoons butter
1 tablespoon oil

Wash and drain the cracked wheat. Bring to the boil 2 pt/1.2 litres water with a little salt, and pour in the grain. Cook with the lid on for 10-15 minutes, until it is tender and the water has been absorbed. You may need to add a little more water. Stir in the butter and oil; let it rest for a few minutes before serving.

VARIATIONS

*If you have meat or chicken stock use it instead of water. It will make the best possible cracked wheat.

*You may add pulses, such as boiled chick-peas and brown lentils, while it is cooking.

*Fried onions and pine nuts are specially good additions. Brown the onions in the butter and oil, add the pine nuts and stir, then add the cracked wheat, water or stock and salt.

Red Lentils and Rice

KETCHRI

This spicy Iraqi dish makes a meal with yogurt. It usually oozes with butter which gives a delicious flavour. But on occasion it is made with oil for serving with meat or chicken. I give the lighter method.

SERVES 6

1 lb/500 g basmati rice
salt
8 oz/250 g red lentils
5 tablespoons oil
2 tablespoons tomato purée
½ teaspoon turmeric
pepper
2 cloves garlic, crushed
3 teaspoons ground cumin

Wash the rice and soak it in salted water for at least 1 hour. Pick over and wash the lentils and drain them both. Heat 2 tablespoons of oil in a heavy bottomed or a non-stick pan, stir in the tomato purée and add 1¾ pt/1 litre water. Add salt, turmeric and pepper, stir well and when it comes to the boil put in the rice and lentils. Cook with the lid on, on the lowest possible heat for 30 minutes.

Fry the garlic quickly in the rest of the oil until it is barely coloured. Stir in the cumin and when the smell rises pour this over the rice and lentils and mix it in with a fork. Steam the rice for another 10 minutes with the lid on, adding more water if necessary.

Lentils and Wheat

MUJADARA BIL BURGHUL

This Syrian dish can be eaten hot or cold (use olive oil if you are going to eat it cold), as an accompaniment to meat or chicken, or as a main dish with yogurt, spring onions, radishes and a Mixed Arab Salad (p. 26).

SERVES 4-6

8 oz/250 g green or brown lentils
salt and pepper
*4 oz/125 g coarse cracked wheat**
1 large Spanish onion, cut in half and thinly sliced
5 tablespoons olive or light vegetable oil

Wash the lentils and remove any stones. Put them in a pan with about 1¼ pt/750 ml water and simmer for 10-15 minutes.

Add salt, pepper and the cracked wheat and cook, covered, on a very low heat for another 15 minutes until the wheat is plump and tender, adding more water if it becomes absorbed too quickly.

In the meantime, fry the onion in 2 tablespoons of oil, stirring constantly, until it is so brown that it is almost caramelized. Stir half of this with the rest of the oil into the lentils and cracked wheat.

Serve garnished with the remaining slices of onion.

CHICK-PEAS AND SPINACH

HUMMUS WA SABANEKH

This vegetable dish may also be made with meat balls. Its flavour comes from the fried garlic and coriander*. This particular flavouring is Egyptian.

SERVES 6

6 oz/175 g chick-peas, soaked for 1 hour
salt
2 lb/1 kg fresh spinach
pepper
4-5 cloves garlic, crushed
1 ½ teaspoons ground coriander
4 tablespoons oil

Boil the drained chick-peas in water for about an hour or more, until they are tender, adding salt when they begin to soften. Keep them covered with water but let it reduce a little, or drain most of it off when they are done.

Wash the spinach thoroughly and remove the thick stems. You can shred the leaves or leave them whole.

Put them in with the chick-peas and stir them in until they soften. Add pepper.

Now make this very Egyptian sauce called taklia. Fry the garlic in oil with the coriander until the aroma rises and stir it into the chick-peas and spinach.

Heat through and serve.

VARIATION

For another less strongly flavoured and colourful version, fry a chopped onion in 2 tablespoons of oil, add the spinach and stir until it crumples into a soft mass.

Sprinkle with salt and pepper and add the boiled and drained chick-peas and 4 peeled and chopped tomatoes. Heat through until the tomatoes soften.

Note: you can use a 14 oz/450 g can of chick-peas. Put them in at the same time as the spinach.

RICE WITH VERMICELLI

ROZ BIL SHAGHRIA

This way of cooking rice is very popular in the Arab world.

SERVES 4

8 oz/250 g long grain rice
4 oz/125 g vermicelli
salt
2 tablespoons butter

Wash and drain the rice.

Break the vermicelli into small pieces with your hands and put it in a tray under the grill. Stir it and let it become brown.

Put ¾ pt/450 ml water to boil with a little salt. Throw in the rice and the vermicelli, stir well and cook with the lid on for 15 minutes or until both are tender and the water has been absorbed. You may need to add a little water whilst cooking.

Stir in the butter and serve.

6
DESSERTS AND PASTRIES

Puddings and pastries are not part of a Middle Eastern meal where the dessert is always fruit. They are for entertaining with tea and coffee and for special occasions. They are made in great quantities during holiday seasons and religious festivals and for weddings, engagements and to celebrate such events as a homecoming, a birth or a first tooth. But there is no reason why you should not serve them as a dessert. I have chosen only a few.

ORANGE SLICES

This is a Moroccan salad.

SERVES 4

6 oranges
*2 tablespoons orange flower water**
3 teaspoons ground cinnamon

Peel the oranges with a sharp knife and remove all the pith, then cut them into thin slices. Arrange on a serving plate. Sprinkle with orange flower water and dust with cinnamon.

FRUIT

FAWAKEH

In every country of the Middle East each daily meal ends with fruit. Often the fruits are cut up so that guests can sample a variety. Few things can be as alluring or give as much pleasure as a large display of fruits of different textures, flavours, shapes and colours – small ones left whole, large ones cut in slices or wedges, some peeled, some not – for people to pick at. The art lies in cutting them up and arranging them in the most beautiful possible manner.

Have an assortment which combines some common fruits, such as apples, pears, plums, apricots or greengages, peaches, cherries, grapes, melon or water melon, with exotic fruits such as figs, persimmons, dates, mangoes, prickly pears, papayas, guavas, lychees and pomegranates. Prepare a bowl of water, acidulated with the juice of 1-2 lemons, so that you can drop in the fruits that discolour for a few minutes when you cut them up. Arrange them on a very large platter on a bed of leaves.

APRICOT DESSERT

Nothing could be easier or more appropriate after a rich meal than this sharp refreshing purée of dried apricots served with a perfumed cream. The only kind of apricots which will do are the slightly acid, orangy brown, very dry variety; the more usual pale moist kind just do not have the right flavour.

SERVES 6

1 lb/500 g dried apricots

1-2 tablespoons sugar (optional)

4 oz/125 g blanched almonds

For the cream

½ pt/300 ml double cream or thick yogurt

1-2 tablespoons sugar

1 tablespoon orange flower or rose water**

Cover the apricots with water and simmer for about 20 minutes or until they are soft and the water is reduced. Put through the blender with their water, adding a little more if necessary to achieve a smooth cream. Add sugar to taste or leave it out. Toast the almonds until slightly coloured and stir them in just before you are ready to serve.

Beat the cream until thick or use the thick or strained yogurt now available and add sugar and orange flower or rose water. Pour over the apricot cream or serve separately.

YOGURT DRINK

LABAN

This is sold in the street in several countries. Vendors now often make it with soda water.

SERVES 4-6

1 pt/600 ml natural yogurt

¾ pt/450 ml water or soda water

salt (optional)

a few sprigs of fresh mint or 2 tablespoons dried crushed mint (optional)

several lumps of ice

Beat the yogurt in a jug, then beat in the water. Add a very little salt, or not, and mint, if you like, and leave for about 10 minutes for the herb to infuse.

A few minutes before you are ready to serve add several lumps of ice.

Dried Fruit Salad

KHOSHAF

In Turkey they say this dish originates in Anatolia where, because of its isolation and lack of transport, the winter diet consists of the summer produce dried in the sun. Dried prunes, apricots, raisins, apples and cherries are boiled up in grape juice and served in the middle of the meal at the same time as rice or cracked wheat*, beans and meat.

But every country has its own version which depends on the fruits and nuts which grow there. It is traditionally made during the month of Ramadan when Muslims fast every day from dawn to sunset.

SERVES 4

8 oz/250 g dried apricots

4 oz/125 g dried prunes

2 oz/50 g currants or sultanas

2 oz/50 g blanched almonds

1 tablespoon pine nuts

1 tablespoon pistachios cut in half

1 tablespoon orange flower, or rose water**

Put all the ingredients together in a serving bowl and leave them to macerate in water, to cover, for 2 days (this gives them a particular quality). Alternatively, simmer for 25 minutes, adding the flower water at the end.

Put a few apricots through the blender with some of the soaking water and return this purée to the bowl to thicken the juice.

Serve chilled.

Couscous with Dried Fruit and Nuts

Serve this filling dessert with cold milk.

SERVES 8

*1 lb/500 g couscous**

3 tablespoons oil

4 oz/125 g dates, pitted and coarsely chopped

2 oz/50 g currants

2 oz/50 g walnuts, coarsely chopped

8 oz/250 g blanched almonds

icing sugar

1 tablespoon ground cinnamon

Put the couscous in a pan with a little less than its volume of water and stir well. Let it absorb the water for 10 minutes, stirring and fluffing it up occasionally to distribute it evenly and to prevent soggy lumps forming.

Add the oil, dates, currants and walnuts, put the lid on and heat up the grain.

Toast the almonds under the grill or in a dry frying pan.

The couscous should be hot, plump and tender when you turn it out onto the serving plate. Shape it into a peaked mountain and cover it entirely with icing sugar.

Draw lines of cinnamon like rays coming out of the peak and stick almonds into the mound all over it.

Accompany by a jug of milk to be served in glasses and by icing sugar in a bowl.

Creamed Rice Pudding

MUHALLABEYA

This version of the most common Arab milk pudding has a honey sauce. The usual one is simply garnished with nuts; another is baked in the oven.

SERVES 6

2 pt/1.2 litres milk
4 oz/125 g ground rice
3 oz/75 g sugar
2-3 tablespoons orange flower or rose water**
3 tablespoons clear honey
3 oz/75 g mixed almonds and pistachios, coarsely chopped

Bring the milk to the boil. Mix the ground rice to a paste with ¼ pt/150 ml water and pour it into the milk, stirring vigorously. Let it come to the boil again slowly over a very low flame, stirring all the time so that lumps do not form (if they do put the whole thing through the blender). Cook until the mixture thickens. Add the sugar and cook, stirring for a few minutes longer, then add the orange flower or rose water and stir well. Pour into a serving dish and let it cool. For the syrup, mix the honey with 4-5 tablespoons of water in a pan and heat it up until it melts. Let it cool before pouring over the cold pudding. Garnish with the nuts.

Saffron Pudding

SHOLEZARD

This delicately coloured and scented rice pudding is Iranian.

SERVES 10

8 oz/250 g short grain rice
3 cardamom pods, cracked
8 oz/250 g sugar
½ teaspoon saffron threads
*3 tablespoons rose water**

For the garnish
2 teaspoons ground cinnamon
1 teaspoon almonds, finely chopped
1 teaspoon pistachios, finely chopped

Put 4 pt/2.4 litres water to boil in a pan. Throw in the rice and cardamom and cook for 30 minutes. Add the sugar and cook for another 15 minutes, stirring occasionally.

Now add the saffron, crushed in a spoon or mortar and diluted in a little water, and cook for about 30 minutes until the rice has disintegrated into a jelly-like cream. Stir in the rose water.

Pour into a serving bowl or individual bowls and garnish with cinnamon, almonds and pistachios, but do not hide all of the brilliant yellow cream.

Serve cold.

Konafa with Cream

KONAFA BIL EISHTA

This is a crisp vermicelli-like pastry filled with a milk and ground rice cream – the oriental equivalent of crème pâtissière – and bathed in a perfumed syrup. It should be eaten hot.

The soft white strands of raw dough, called konafa or kadaif are bought ready-made in 1 lb/500 g bags from the same stores who make fillo*.

SERVES 10 OR MORE

1 lb/500 g konafa

8 oz/250 g unsalted butter, melted

For the filling

4 tablespoons ground rice

4 tablespoons cornflour

2½ pt/1.5 litres milk

5 tablespoons sugar

2 tablespoons rose or orange flower water**

8 oz/250 g blanched almonds, finely chopped (optional)

For the syrup

1 lb/500 g sugar

½ pt/300 ml water

1 tablespoon lemon juice

2 tablespoons rose or orange flower water* or 1 tablespoon of each*

For the garnish

3 oz/75 g pistachios, finely chopped

First make the cream filling. Mix the ground rice and cornflour to a paste with a little of the milk. Then bring the rest of the milk to the boil in a pan with the sugar.

Beat some of it into the paste and pour this back into the pan. Let it simmer, stirring constantly so that lumps do not form (if they do, put the whole thing through the blender) until the mixture thickens.

Be careful not to let it burn at the bottom of the pan. Remove from the heat and add the rose or orange flower water and stir in the almonds, if used.

Now put the raw konafa into a large bowl and pour the melted and slightly cooled butter over it.

Pull out and separate the strands and mix them well with your hands, so that they do not stick together and so that they are thoroughly coated with butter.

Spread half of this pastry evenly over the bottom of a large round tray or ovenproof dish, pour the cream filling evenly over it and cover with a layer of the remaining pastry.

Press down firmly with your hands so that it all holds together compactly.

Bake in a moderate gas 4/350°F/180°C oven for 45 minutes, then turn up the oven to gas 8/450°F/230 °C and bake for 15 minutes longer, or until it is a light golden colour.

Prepare the syrup as soon as you put the pastry in the oven (or before), so that it has time to cool. Boil the sugar and water with the lemon juice (this stops the syrup from crystallizing when it is cold) for about 10 minutes until it is thick enough to coat a spoon, then add the orange flower or rose water, and simmer for ½ minute longer. Let it cool, then put it in the refrigerator for a while to chill.

When you are ready to serve, cut around the pastry with a sharp knife and turn out onto a large round serving plate, pour the syrup all over and sprinkle with pistachios.

Note: you may serve it in the tray if you find it easier and you can use less syrup if you don't like it as sweet.

VARIATIONS

Konafa bil loz has a nut filling and should be eaten cold. Instead of the cream filling use:

*2 lb/1 kg ground or finely chopped walnuts mixed with 2 tablespoons cinnamon and 3 tablespoons sugar.

*Or 2 lb/1 kg minced or very finely chopped almonds (if you would like to try an Iraqi flavouring mix with 2 teaspoons ground cardamom).

*Or 2 lb/1 kg minced or finely chopped pistachios.

Moroccan Almond Snake

M'HENCHA

M'hencha means snake. It looks beautiful and tastes wonderful and you can make it as large as you like. Fillo* can be used instead of the Moroccan pancake-like pastry called ouarka. The measures here are enough for a large party.

SERVES 30

3 lb/1.5 kg ground almonds

2 lb/1 kg caster sugar

2 tablespoons ground cinnamon

*7-8 fl oz/200-250 ml orange flower water**

*1 lb/500 g fillo pastry**

3-4 oz/75-125 g butter, melted

2 egg yolks

To garnish

icing sugar

1 tablespoon cinnamon

For the filling, mix ground almonds, sugar, cinnamon and orange flower water (just enough for it to be like moist sand) and work into a paste with your hands.

Take the sheets of fillo out only when you are ready to start, and keep them in a stack while you are working, as they dry out quickly.

Brush the top sheet lightly with butter. Take lumps of the almond paste, roll into fingers and place them end to end on the sheet so as to have a line as thick as a fat thumb about 1 in/2.5 cm from the long edge.

Roll the pastry up tightly over the almond filling. Press the ends of the roll towards the centre, like an accordion, so that it becomes crinkled (this ensures that the pastry does not tear when you curve it round). Lift the roll up very carefully and place it on a large sheet of foil (it will make it easier for you to slide it off later) on a large oven tray.

Starting from the centre of the tray, curve the almond-filled roll into a tight coil. Repeat with the rest of the fillo until all the filling is used up and place the rolls end to end to make a long curled-up snake.

Brush the top of the pastry with the egg yolks beaten with 1 tablespoon of water and bake in a gas 4/350°F/180°C oven for about 45 minutes or until crisp and brown.

Dust with icing sugar and sprinkle lines of cinnamon in the shape of a cross, or whatever you like.

You can serve it hot, but I think it is better cold.

Turkish Coffee

KAHWA

Turkish coffee is drunk black and sweetened (it does not have to be too sweet) in little demitasse cups. The long handled cylindrical pots used for making it come in different sizes. You can buy them large enough to make one, two, three or four cups.

You can use any kind of coffee in a darkish roast providing that it is pulverised – that is ground to the finest powder.

SERVES 1

1 heaped teaspoon pulverised coffee

1 teaspoon sugar, or to taste

Pour a small coffee cupful of water into the pot. Add coffee and sugar, stir well and put on the fire. Remove as soon as it begins to rise, lift the froth with a little spoon and drop it into the cup (this saves the maximum froth and when you are making several cups ensures that everyone gets their share of it). Give the coffee a stir and let it come to the boil again before pouring.

Note: this is the Turkish way. In Arab countries they boil the water first (sometimes with a cardamom pod), add the rest and bring to the boil – usually three times.

GLOSSARY

Coriander
This can be a spice or a herb. The green herb is sold fresh in bunches. It looks very much like flat-leaved parsley. It wilts quickly and should be kept in the refrigerator or with its stalks in water. The green leaves are never dried. The spice is a little round seed which is sold whole or ready-ground. It cannot be used instead of the fresh green leaves which have a completely different taste.

Couscous
Hard wheat which has been coarsely ground then moistened and rolled in flour. It is cooked by steaming. The couscous found in this country is pre-cooked and only needs soaking in ¾ or more (see instructions on the packet) of its volume of water and heating through (usually with a little salt and a few tablespoons of butter or oil). The name couscous is also given to the whole dish – the grain and the garnish or stew.

Cracked wheat
Burghul in Arabic, bulgur in Turkish and it is called pourgouri in Cyprus. You can find all these names on packets available here. It is wheat which has been boiled and dried then ground to a fine or coarse texture. It can be served like rice, plain or with other ingredients in a pilaf. It is quick and easy to use and versatile. For most cooked dishes the coarsely ground cracked wheat is best, but use the finely ground grain for tabbouleh and kibbeh. For basic preparation, see p. 27 and p. 77.

Dried limes
Noumi Basra or Oman lemons are limes which have been dried until they are brown, sound hollow and the inside becomes a very dark brown. They have a delicious and unusual sour musty flavour. They are sold whole or ground and you can make them yourself by leaving limes to dry out on a radiator. It takes months, depending on the size of the limes. They are good in soups and stews. You can put them in whole and pierce them with a fork when they soften, or crack them open.

Fillo
This is also spelt phylo (I have previously called it fila as we did in Egypt) and is paper-thin dough. The sheets are sold fresh and frozen in 1 lb/500 g airtight

packets. They dry out quickly and must be taken out of the packet only when they are ready to be used.

Harissa

This is a fiery red pepper paste used in North Africa and more particularly in Tunisia where people put it in everything (even spread on bread for breakfast).

Mergez

Spicy North African sausages.

Orange flower water

The distilled essence of the petals which is sold here is very diluted. It gives a delicate scent to all kinds of sweet dishes. You can put a few drops in cold or hot water to make a soothing drink.

Pomegranate syrup

Boiled down juice of the sour (not sweet) fruit.

Preserved lemons or limes

Preserved in salt, these are a speciality of North Africa where they are used in all kinds of dishes. To make them, wash the lemons well and cut them in 4 – in 2 if they are limes – but not right through, and let them hold together at the stem. Sprinkle salt inside the slits. Use 2 oz/50 g for 1 lb/500 g lemons and press them down in a jar. When their juices are released and they begin to soften, press them down with a weight. Add extra lemon juice so that they are entirely covered to preserve them. They should be ready to use, soft and mellow within 1 month. Use 1 or 2, chopped up (it is usual to remove the pulp and use only the peel).

Rose water

The distilled essence of rose petals. The kind which is sold here is diluted. It is used to perfume desserts and pastries. It is also supposed to be good for the skin and people wash their faces with it. A soothing drink, to take before you go to sleep, is made by adding a few drops with a tiny bit of sugar to hot or cold water.

Sumac

A dark reddish-brown seed which has an unusual sharp flavour. It is used instead of lemon, either sprinkled on food in its ground form or infused in water and then strained.

Tahina

The oily paste of crushed sesame seeds.

Tamarind

A fibrous pod from which can be extracted a wonderful sour juice after soaking in boiling water. You can buy tamarind paste which is much easier to use.

INDEX